Data Analytics

The Ultimate Guide to Big Data Analytics for Business, Data Mining Techniques, Data Collection, and Business Intelligence Concepts

© **Copyright 2018**

All rights Reserved. No part of this book may be reproduced in any form without permission in writing from the author. Reviewers may quote brief passages in reviews.

Disclaimer: No part of this publication may be reproduced or transmitted in any form or by any means, mechanical or electronic, including photocopying or recording, or by any information storage and retrieval system, or transmitted by email without permission in writing from the publisher.

While all attempts have been made to verify the information provided in this publication, neither the author nor the publisher assume any responsibility for errors, omissions or contrary interpretations of the subject matter herein.

Any persons or organizations referred to herein are composites for the purpose of illustration and do not represent real persons or organizations.

This book is for entertainment purposes only. The views expressed are those of the author alone, and should not be taken as expert instruction or commands. The reader is responsible for his or her own actions.

Adherence to all applicable laws and regulations, including international, federal, state and local laws governing professional licensing, business practices, advertising and all other aspects of doing business in the US, Canada, UK or any other jurisdiction is the sole responsibility of the purchaser or reader.

Neither the author nor the publisher assumes any responsibility or liability whatsoever on the behalf of the purchaser or reader of these materials. Any perceived slight of any individual or organization is purely unintentional.

Contents

INTRODUCTION 1

CHAPTER 1: OVERVIEW OF DATA ANALYTICS: WHAT IS DATA ANALYTICS (AND BIG DATA ANALYTICS)? 3

CHAPTER 2: DATA ANALYTICS AND BUSINESS INTELLIGENCE 6

BUSINESS INTELLIGENCE (BI) 6
    Data analytics 7

THE BUSINESS INTELLIGENCE TOOLS 8
    Looker 9
    GoodData 10
    Tableau 11
    KISSmetrics 12
    Cyfe 13
    Similarweb Pro 14
    Woopra 15

CHAPTER 3: DATA ANALYSIS AND DATA ANALYTICS 18

CHAPTER 4: DATA MINING 21

CHAPTER 5: DATA COLLECTION 26

THE METHODS OF DATA COLLECTION, AND BIG DATA 26
THE TYPES OF DATA 27

CHAPTER 6: TYPES OF DATA ANALYTICS 29

DESCRIPTIVE ANALYTICS (WHAT HAPPENED) 29
DIAGNOSTIC ANALYTICS (WHAT MADE IT OCCUR?) 29
PREDICTIVE ANALYTICS (WHAT'S GOING TO OCCUR?) 30

PRESCRIPTIVE ANALYTICS (WHAT TO DO) 31

CHAPTER 7: THE PROCESS: THE LIFECYCLE OF BIG DATA ANALYTICS 33

1: THE EVALUATION OF BUSINESS CASE 35
2: IDENTIFICATION OF DATA 37
3: THE ACQUISITION OF DATA, AND FILTERING 39
4: THE EXTRACTION OF DATA 41
5: VALIDATION AND CLEANSING OF THE DATA 43
6: AGGREGATION AND REPRESENTATION OF DATA 45
7: DATA ANALYSIS 48
8: VISUALIZATION OF DATA 50
9: UTILIZATION OF THE ANALYSIS RESULTS 52

CHAPTER 8: BEHAVIORAL ANALYTICS: USING BIG DATA ANALYTICS TO FIND HIDDEN CUSTOMER BEHAVIOR PATTERNS 59

CHAPTER 9: FURTHER PATTERN DISCOVERY IN ADVANCED ANALYTICS: MACHINE LEARNING 63

CONCLUSION 69

PART 2: DATA MINING 70

THE DATA MINING GUIDE FOR BEGINNERS, INCLUDING APPLICATIONS FOR BUSINESS, DATA MINING TECHNIQUES, CONCEPTS, AND MORE 70

INTRODUCTION 71

CHAPTER 1: OVERVIEW OF DATA MINING 72

CHAPTER 2: KNOW YOUR DATA 82

CHAPTER 3: DATA PREPARATION 85

CHAPTER 4: SIMILARITY AND DISTANCES 96

CHAPTER 5: ASSOCIATION PATTERN MINING 106

CHAPTER 6: CLUSTER ANALYSIS 112

CHAPTER 7: OUTLIER ANALYSIS 121

CHAPTER 8: DATA CLASSIFICATION 126

CHAPTER 9: APPLICATIONS OF DATA MINING IN BUSINESS 133

CHAPTER 10: THE BEST DATA MINING TECHNIQUES TO USE 136

CONCLUSION 140

Part 1: Data Analytics

An Essential Beginner's Guide To Data Mining, Data Collection, Big Data Analytics For Business, And Business Intelligence Concepts

Introduction

This book has lots of valuable eye opening information about data analytics, which will help you understand the concept of data mining, data collection, big data analytics for business and business intelligence concepts.

As you may already know, the concept of data analytics has been with us for many years. This special practice that has evolved from 'simple forms' and matured to what many call 'an integral part of the world of business'. Most organizations now understand pretty much that they need better ways to capture all data streaming into their business and they find it hard to avoid applying modern data analytics for the significance and value it offers.

Data analytics, which basically refers to the process by which you examine data sets in order to derive conclusions about the information they contain (largely with assistance of software and specialized systems), started being used as far back as the 1950s. During this time, nobody could even utter the term 'big data' even though at the most basic level (generally numbers in a spreadsheet that were examined manually), data analytics was carried out to unearth insights and trends.

Understanding data analytics is important because for one:

Many serious businesses today look to apply data analytics to improve efficiency and speed. Unlike in the past where business owners had to uncover information and gather information to use for future decisions, a business, today, can pinpoint insights for instant decisions. You will thus have to appreciate that what makes data analytics important and prevalent is its capacity to work faster, remain agile, and the fact that it tends to offer organizations a competitive edge which they never had before. Big data analytics in particular also enables organizations in harnessing their data and use it to find or identify new opportunities. This in turn leads to niftier business moves, operations that are more efficient, more profits and more satisfied customers.

With this book, not only will you understand all the internal nitty-gritties about data analytics, you will also understand why data analytics is changing the business arena. You'll realize that the high-performance analytics will enable you to do stuff that you never thought about before probably because the volumes of data were just too big (among other reasons) and so much more.

We'll begin by first examining what data analytics really means and what it entails. Do not fret when you meet challenging terms as you read on, as I will try to include a detailed explanation of each one of them. Let's begin.

Chapter 1: Overview Of Data Analytics: What Is Data Analytics (And Big Data Analytics)?

Data analytics has no single, standard meaning but at this point, you can look at it simply as the quest to extract meaning from raw data by use of specialized computer systems. These systems essentially organize, transform and model the data in order to draw conclusions and trace patterns.

Data analytics can be simple and today, the term is used majorly to describe the analysis of high-velocity data or large volumes of data, which in itself offers unique challenges regarding computation and data handling. The skilled professionals in data analytics, who generally have a deep proficiency in statistics are known as data scientists.

Moreover, while data analytics also involves *big data* processing, I wouldn't say it is only meant for big data (like many people believe) because it is only a general term we use for any processing type that reviews historical data over time. However, the term 'data analytics' is indeed evolving to favor large data-capable systems as the size of organizational data keeps growing.

But what is big data?

In case you are wondering, the term 'big data' refers to data whose size is indeterminate, is increasing steadily, and this data is coming from a number of sources that are largely indeterminate, including the data generated from partners, employees, machines, customers, databases, mobile devices, logs, mobile devices, security cameras, social media among others.

Big data is generally characterized by at least one (but often all) of these characteristics:

- Massive volume- this means that big data is large, and usually adds up to terabytes and sometimes petabyte; its growth is so high that it becomes difficult to have a precise calculation.

- High velocity- most of the data in business today changes constantly. For instance, the stock market prices change multiple times each second. In this regard, big data addresses the problem of capturing and analyzing data, which is at continuous flux.

- Variety- in the Information technology context, the term data at one time mainly meant relational data that is stored in databases. In contrast, big data involves any and all the data types, irrespective of how it was actually created. The non-relational data is usually known as *unstructured data.* It encompasses things which businesses once didn't have any insight on- for instance, audio, email, social media and so forth.

Therefore, big data is a problem.

The amount of data that is generated keeps increasing by the second, and so the challenge to control or keep in check this 'big data' is undeniably a moving target. What's more, big data is becoming more and more a *competitive problem*. As more companies invest in and have success in managing their big data, the companies that fail to keep step remain at a great disadvantage. Today, commercial products and companies that contain and control big data are emerging and evolving really fast as this problem is increasingly proving to be a great opportunity.

How has big data affected data analytics therefore?

The administrators in the world of relational databases generated reports easily on the contents of data for business use, but these only provided very minute or limited business intelligence (explained in the next subtopic). In this case, they used data warehouses (data warehousing is the technology which totals structured data from a single or multiple sources to be compared and analyzed for improved business intelligence) but these generally cannot be able to manage the scale of big data cost efficiently.

NOTE: Even as data warehouses remain to be a relevant form of data analytics, data analytics seems to be gradually getting a specific connotation with respect to the problem of analyzing data of high velocity, volume and variety.

We thus have something called big data analytics, which is the process of examining varied and large sets of data (i.e. big data) to uncover market trends, hidden patterns, customer preferences, unknown correlations, and other important information in this regard that can assist businesses to make decisions that are more informed.

We'll talk more about big data analytics in a moment.

Data analytics is the core of the current business enterprise

Businesses across the globe are facing growing complexity and volatility in the market. In response, all business functions are resorting to insights and data-driven analytics as a way to manage this growing uncertainty, while better understanding the customer bases of their organizations and growing their businesses.

You also need to appreciate that continued business reliance on technology, which includes automation, is forcing this move to data-driven insights. The constant growth in digital technologies is driving the capacity to analyze more data, which is in turn, fueling the appetite of the enterprise to get better data, better or more advanced skills in analytics and the execution of best practices. The key enabler to develop meaning and truth from data that drives business growth is analytics.

Before we talk about the types of data analytics and big data, let's take a look at some concepts related to data analytics

Chapter 2: Data Analytics And Business Intelligence

There is a strong overlap existing between business intelligence and data analytics, which is evident by the fact that many people use the two terms interchangeably. It is not uncommon to find most industry experts grouping the two terms together but since I'm sure you are serious about changing data into practical insights, I have to differentiate them for you.

While most of enterprise organizations like deploying one alongside the other, the two processes are very different, and without a doubt, you cannot practice one successfully without the other one. We'll break each one of them down so that we have a clearer focus.

Business intelligence (BI)

There are different ways to look at BI. One of them is that Business intelligence is the procedural and technical infrastructure that stores and analyzes company data (from its activities) after collecting it. BI is a broad term that covers things like process analysis, data mining, descriptive analysis and performance benchmarking. BI is meant to take in all the data a business generates and present performance measures that are easy to digest, and also trends that may inform management decisions.

To further break down the concept, you need to note that:

Business intelligence emerged from a conviction that managers with incomplete or inaccurate information will tend (on average) to make decisions that are worse than those they would make if they had more information. Financial model creators will look at this as some sort of 'garbage in, garbage out' issue. Business intelligence is essentially meant to solve this problem by introducing the most recent data that is ideally presented in quick metrics dashboard intended to support better decisions.

If, for instance, you are in charge of production schedules for a number of beverage factories and the sales are depicting robust month-over-month growth in some region, you can approve additional shifts in near real time to make sure your factories are able to meet the demand.

Likewise, you can idle down the same production quickly if you realize that a cooler than normal summer is impacting sales. This is a just a limited case of how business intelligence can grow profits and reduce costs when you use it well.

Business intelligence, to be useful, has to look to increase the timelines, accuracy and the amount of data. This means finding additional ways to capture information that is not already being recorded, inspecting the information for possible errors and structuring it in a way that makes broad analysis possible. Nonetheless, when it comes to practice, companies have data coming in unstructured or varied formats that don't allow for simple collection and analysis. Therefore, the software firms come in to provide business intelligence solutions. These are the enterprise level software applications made to unify data and analytics of a company.

Looked at differently, and perhaps with more relativeness to data analytics, we can also say that:

Business intelligence is the process of using data to make business decisions. BI is an umbrella term that refers to data use in a predictive environment. Business intelligence covers analytics, and acts as the non-technical sister or parallel term that is used to define this process. Usually, BI refers to the process companies use to learn from the data they're collecting, after analyzing it. Equally, you can use business intelligence to describe the tools, plans and strategies that are involved with decision making that is data-driven.

Data analytics

Analytics on the other hand is simply a data science; if BI is the portion of decision making, then Data Analytics is the process used to ask questions. When your company wants to try and forecast what will occur in future, you use analytics tools; you'll then use business intelligence tools to transform these forecasts and predictive models into common language. In the current data heavy marketplace, we use analytics solutions to provide descriptions of the ways a user can break down the data and look at the trends occurring over time. In short, you set up an initiative of business intelligence, but *do/conduct* data analytics.

Therefore, I would say that data analytics is how you get BI. The process of analytics, regardless of how long it takes, is what brings a business owner to a place where he can make predictions accurately about what will occur in the future, and that is what makes his business 'intelligent.' You can think of data analytics as the question-answering phase that leads up to the decision making phase in the whole scheme of business intelligence.

Just to get a better understanding of Business Intelligence, we'll try to delve deeper into it; let's take a look at the tools used in BI.

The Business Intelligence tools

The following list contains the most popular BI tools used today. As you read through, know that the more advanced the system is, the more data sources it is capable of combining, and this includes the internal metrics that come from various company departments, and the external data extracted from social media channels, third party systems, emails or macroeconomic data. As you will eventually realize, business intelligence software assists companies have a better insight on their general growth, customer behavior and sales trends.

Domo

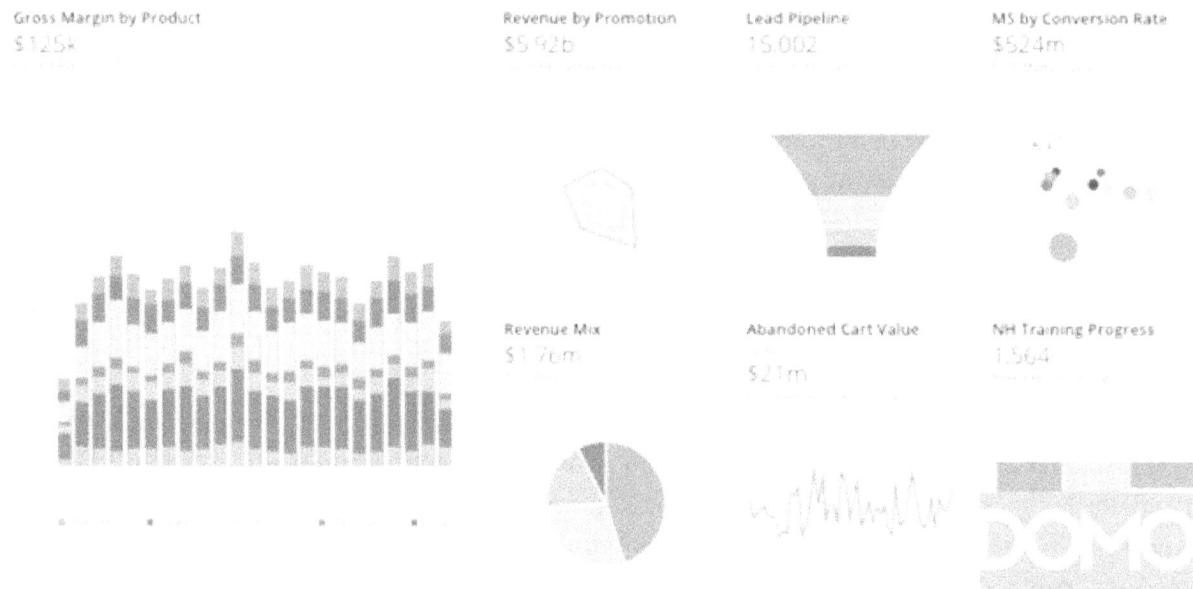

This is one of the best BI tools, which stands out because it offers the widest dataset and also connector support. With Domo, you can use one single dashboard to look at data in real time. The interface of the system, dashboards widgets and displays are very attractive. Domo is also known to offer understandable visualizations of BI and data that you can get actionable insights from to make smart moves. For instance, you can connect the page view numbers you gathered from Google analytics for specific products and measure the items' influence.

The main features of Domo include mobile optimization, project management, messaging and communication, appstore, business data connection options and flexible integration. By using Domo, you are sure to get important insights on the interests, behavior and conversation of your followers on social media and fans as well. Since the site has been optimized for mobile use, this essentially means that you can generate reports using your smartphone with a lot of ease. There is a free starter plan containing basic features that small businesses can utilize. For the larger organizations that have more generous budgets, there are the paid packages beginning from $175 per month.

Looker

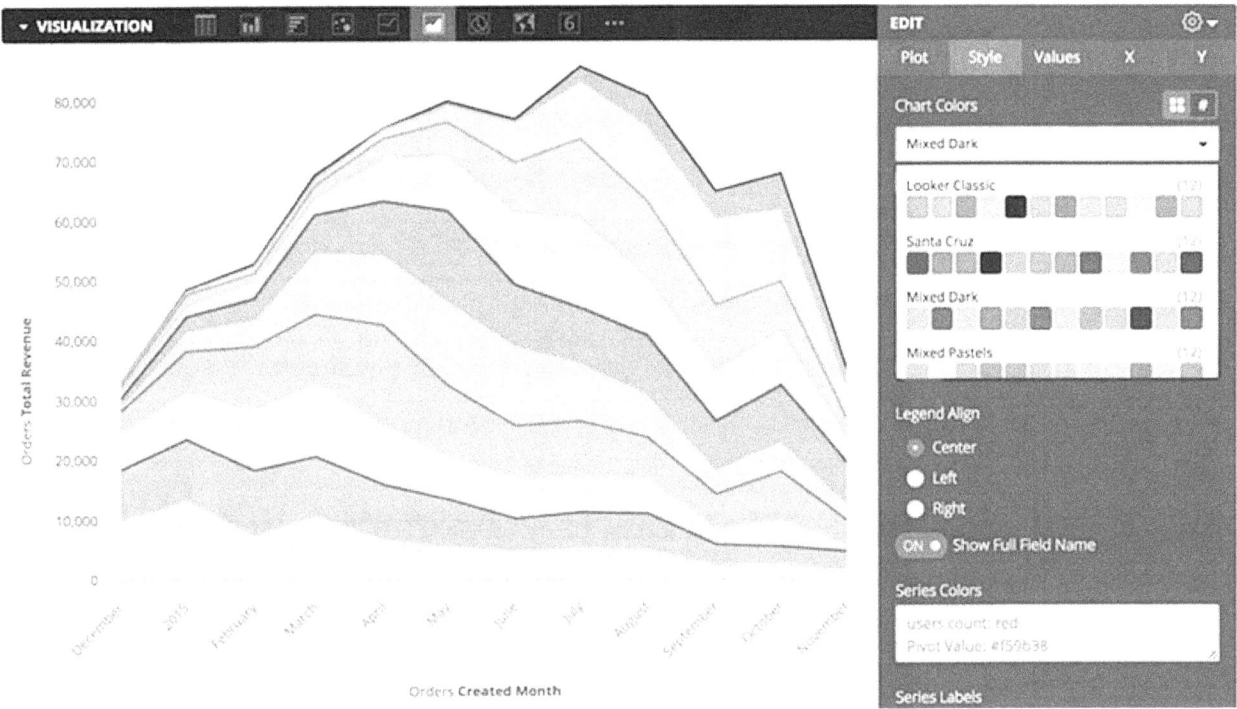

If you want to make effective use of this tool, all you require is a little bit of SQL knowledge. Just by using basic coding skills, you can create your own design visualizations and analytic modules easily. Even if you don't have SQL knowledge, you can learn from the vast library of useful lectures of the product, live recordings, videos and training materials. The documentation you get also provides interactive puzzles, which contribute to make analytics a really fun activity. A noteworthy highlight is that this platform analyzes both web-hosted information and SQL and houses more than 25 variations of data such as Vertica, BigQuery and Hive.

Among the top features of this tool includes collaboration tools, the drag and drop mechanism, browser-based interface, customizable and exportable graphs, reports and charts, and also APIs (Application Programing Interface- it refers to the set of subroutine protocols, tools and definitions used to build app software) for integration. In fact, even the lay users in your organization will be able to utilize the app to make data-rich visualizations and dashboards. You can share reports and data effortlessly through email and URLs by using the collaboration tools, and consolidate them with custom and third party solutions. Lastly, the pricing is generally quote based and you receive live tech support.

GoodData

If you want a cloud analytics solution that is user-friendly and provides important features like marketing, sales and service analytics templates, dynamic charts and graphs, agile data warehousing service, ad-hoc reporting and real time access, then GoodData should probably be your best choice. The best thing about this tool is that it isolates practicable insights that can improve the agility and health of your company. You can also use it to boost budget and resources smartly, predictability and make faster decisions.

The complete package of GoodData includes analytics and sophisticated visualizations, data discovery, self-service, data warehousing and data ready-ETL (Extract, Transform and Load- refers to the process of extracting data from external sources, transforming it to fit operational needs and then loading it into the data warehouse or end target database) or ELT (Extract, Load, Transform- this is the process of extracting data from the source, loading it into the target data warehouse or target database).

You can also use this tool to unearth the customer insights that can assist you measure the effectiveness of your marketing campaigns and also operational insights to assist you make smarter decisions. On top of that, you can utilize the embedded functionality of analytics to pinpoint prospects for fresh revenue streams. What's more, through multiple channels, you can count on expert customer support. Just contact the vendor to get a custom quote to get these benefits.

Tableau

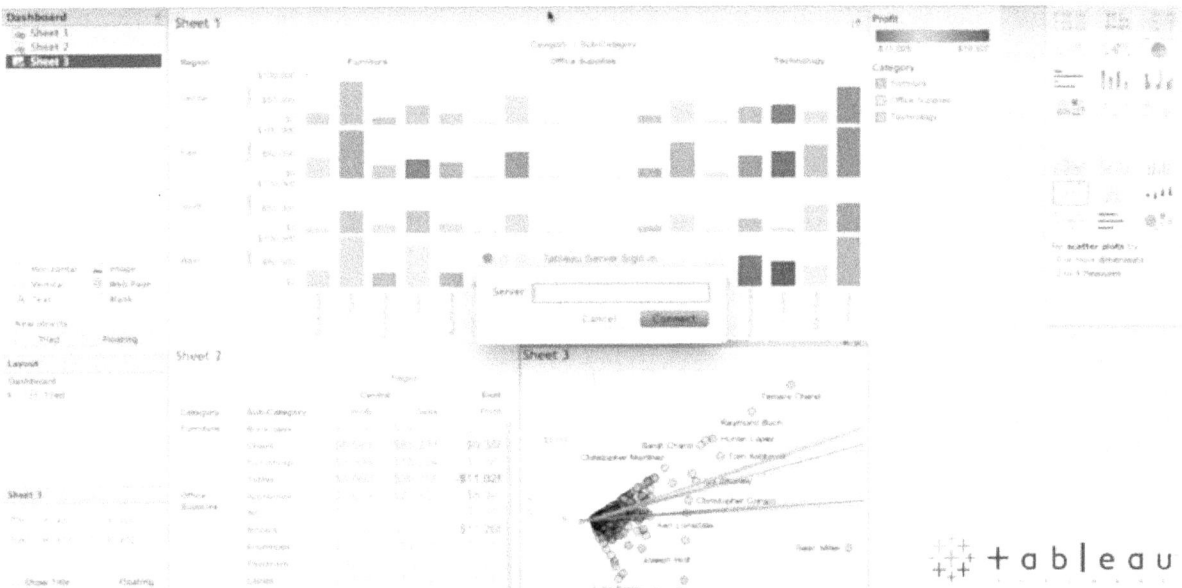

Without a doubt, tableau is one of the best BI solutions and is popular due to its ease of use and robustness. You can use this tool to understand, visualize and share your data easily. I personally like this tool because it doesn't require you to have any programming skills to make, publish and share dashboards. What's more, this system is self-service analytics based and offers quick answers to simple as well as complex queries. Some of its best features include server **REST API**, dashboard for commenting, automatic updates, security permissions at all levels and mobile-ready dashboards.

When you invest in Tableau, you gain several benefits, which include collaboration tools to enable group analytics which it essentially provides, the fact that you leverage the public dashboard easily to access and analyze data and also the fact that you can deploy this application on the local servers or in the cloud. The pricing is affordable and begins from $35 per month (per user) but is billed annually. Lastly, the tool automates data updates- this means that businesses can receive the most recent information without experiencing delays.

KISSmetrics

This one is a very robust BI system, which makes it possible to identify, track and enhance important business metrics. You can change this information into practicable insights and use them to make effective strategies in marketing and enhance marketing practices. One of its features that stand out is deep tracking. This provides good customer insights, which enables you to understand the intentions and behaviors of your customers even before they buy your service or product. The other main features include the following: unlimited retention reports, unlimited customer profiles, no-limit conversion periods, data export and unlimited A/B test reports.

(A/B testing or split testing refers to the process whereby you compare 2 version of a given web page in order to determine the one that performs better. By showing the two variants –you can call them A and B- you can then proceed to compare 2 web pages to the same visitors simultaneously. The best one is automatically the one that offers a conversion rate that is far much better.)

According to me though, the best part about this tool is the fact that it centers on people and tracks the shifts of customers and trends, and interprets the overall business health of an organization. Moreover, it keeps stock of the details of all prospects and customers who are in contact with your business. This information is important as you can use it to make targeted marketing campaigns. The pricing packages of Kissmetrics are $220 per month (the self-service plan), $500 per month for the growth plan and $700 per month for the power plan.

Cyfe

Cyfe is basically a dashboard application we use to track and make an analysis of data strewn across existing services like Google Analytics and Salesforce. Your clients can use the dashboard to look at real time data and remain in the loop. The good thing is that you can share information securely and instantly, and reduce the reports you submit to your clients. Its main features include the following: historical data, track individual departments, white labeling, pre-built integrations and real time reports.

One of the key benefits of Cyfe is that it provides you with in-depth insights on your SEM, SEO, web analytics, social media profiles, email marketing channels and so on. What's more, you are able to monitor many different websites. Cyfe is also popular because of its flawless reporting functionality, which can allow you to make a summary of the data on the dashboards, compare it and share it with other people. You'll also find TV mode also great for meetings as it makes it possible for you to automatically rotate dashboards on the big screen monitor. This tool comes with a forever free plan that small businesses and startups can benefit from. The paid premium package on the other hand goes for $19 per month (billed monthly) or $14 per month (billed annually).

Similarweb Pro

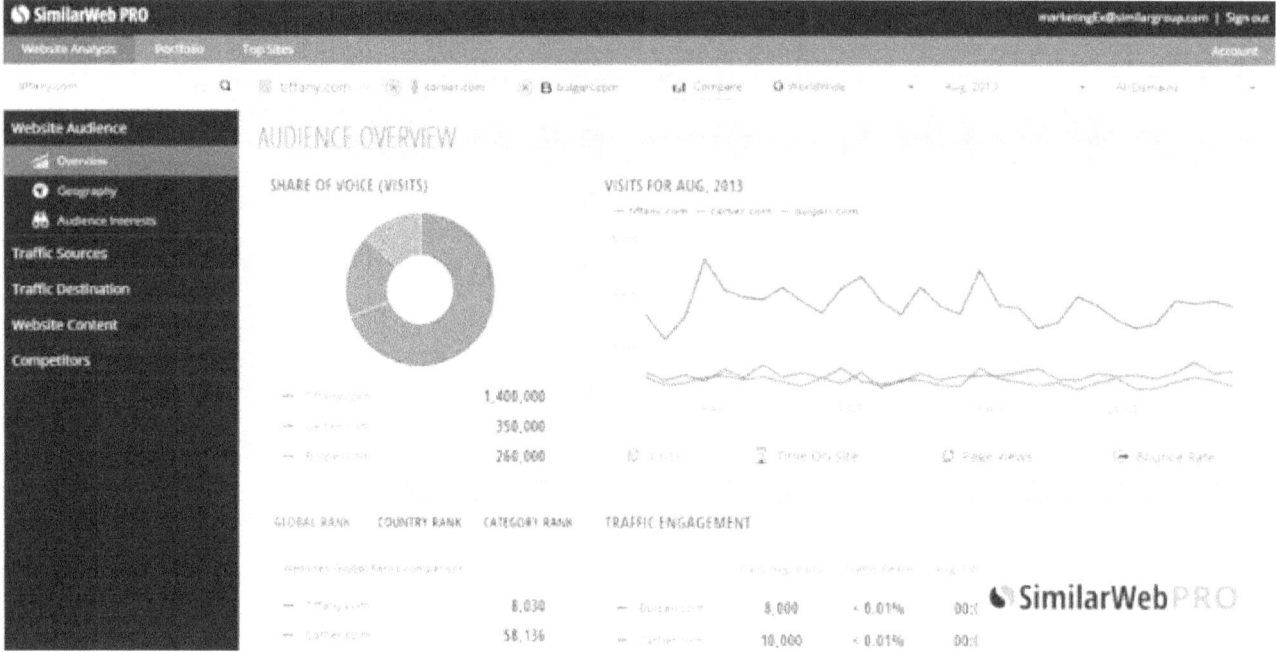

This tool offers effective website analytics tools that you can use to find out the traffic statistics of your sites. This is particularly great if you want to create strategies in order to get more traffic in your sites. Essentially, you can also compare the performance of your competitors' website with yours. Its top features include mobile app traffic sources, a comprehensive keyword analysis, email traffic reports, visual graphs and charts for KPIs.

If you have a large organization, you can take advantage of this tool for your merger and acquisition strategies and also marketing efforts. The main benefit of this tool is that it assists you analyze any industry or website out there. Other advantages include: multi-user access, custom reporting, the loads of API integration and professional support. The vendor will offer you a free plan that has the basic features and also two quote-priced packages.

Woopra is the customer analytics tool that we use to understand the activities of our customers and behavior across different touch points, which include email, helpdesk and live chat. This tool creates comprehensive profiles for the customers by tracking their activity on web and mobile, and syncs information from multiple sources. It then updates the profiles in real time automatically. Its main features include scheduled tasks, real time data and analytics.

You can use the customer profiles and segments of Woopra to make analytical custom reports, funnel reports and retention reports. The solution sends notifications in real time to your mobile or desktop application when customers perform noteworthy actions. With this tool, you can easily understand customer behavior and utilize the insights to generate data-driven strategies instead of just depending on guesswork. The app is basically free to use for small businesses for up to 30,000 actions per month. The pricing begins from $79.95 (billed monthly) or $799.50 (billed yearly) for up to 400,000 actions per month. If you have a big enterprise, you can contact the vendor for a custom quote.

Other tools include the following:

Sisense

Just as it is a winner of last year's best business intelligence software award from *FinancesOnline*, Sisense is one of the leaders in the Business intelligence market. Sisense is a solution that is able to effectively simplify data analyses that are complex, and then make big data insights to be accessible even for small companies and startups. Why does Sisense have such a competitive edge? The reason lies in its capabilities to collate data from many different sources without the usual pricey preparations (these sources include Google Analytics, Salesforce and AdWords- among others). As a user of Sisense, you also get to enjoy the capacity of the tool to use in-chip technology efficiently in a database that processes data ten times quicker than traditional systems. Sisense also works a technology known as ElastiCube that is very innovative- this means that it able to import big data sets and work with any given CPU layout without negatively affecting the quality of the results. For more information about its features, you can try out the software yourself, perhaps first with the free trial plan they are offering. Just click **here** to sign up for the free trial.

Actuate Business Intelligence and Reporting Tools (BIRT)

This tool is commonly valued for its nature of being flexible, 100% pure Java and open source and is thus used for creating and publishing reports against sources of data that range from XML data sources to typical business relational databases and in-memory Java objects. This tool, which leverages the rich abilities of the eclipse platform is developed as a top-level project inside the Eclipse foundation; it also leverages on an active open source users community. Developers in all levels can include robust reporting into their Java, Eclipse-based applications and J2EE.

icCube

This tool is a SaaS (Software as a Service- refers to a distribution model of software which third party providers hosts apps and avails them to customers through the internet) end to end Business Intelligence platform; it is specialized to be fixed or embedded in your application. You can set it up in the cloud, on premises or just choose to use one of their managed services to enjoy a limited period to market for the custom feature requests. As you will realize, it integrates flawlessly with any given application due to the on-the-fly authorization and authentication, its ability to connect and bring together any custom source of data, direct access to R and Java (R refers to the graphics and statistical computing open source programming language -and software environment- supported by the R foundation; it is a dashboard builder that is web based and the capacity to design widgets graphically from ground up. If you are a software developer who wants to provide a solid web-based self-service Business Intelligence solution or predefined dashboards to your end users, icCube is bound to be your dream tool.

I'm sure you are now more conversant with the term business intelligence, and how it compares to data analytics. We'll now take another brief overview of another confounding issue in business-data analysis –, its relationship with data analytics and perhaps how the two terms differ.

Chapter 3: Data Analysis And Data Analytics

Before we begin, and so that we are on the same page, you need to note the following:

As you may have realized already, businesses are currently relying on data to get quantified insights that lead to positive business outcomes. By use of data, the 'guess work' in business approach is taken out and is replaced with hard facts which can make the process of decision making more efficient. When you consider that folks are making more than 2.5 quintillion bytes of data each day, it's really not a surprise that 'data' has refused to leave most people's lips. This data, according to ICD, is expected to grow ten-fold and by 2020, will expectedly cross about 44 zettabytes. The **report** according to ICD also asserted that the amount of useful data will escalate from 22% to 35% by 2020. The explosion of data is only going to rise as the total number of smartphone-users increase around the world.

We can expect to witness over 50 billion connected smartphones over the succeeding five years; and as we keep marveling at this explosion of data, we have to state that data is nothing more than data unless it's made to work. It's only when this is done that business gains the advantage it promises to offer.

Data analysis and data analytics are some of those terms that have been used interchangeably for a very long time. But at least we know that analysis and analytics assist convert data into practical insights that provide business value. While these terms might sound similar, they are quite different. Both analytics and analysis definitely make it possible to have decision making that is evidence-based by revealing patterns and opportunities lying inside the data but their approach to the data is where the difference lies. Simply put, one of them looks towards the past and the other looks towards the future.

According to experts, data analysis is the hands-on exploration and evaluation of data. It refers to the process of transforming, cleaning, modelling and inspecting data with a goal of getting useful information, supporting decision making and suggesting conclusions. Data analysis thus has different approaches and facets, which encompass diverse techniques under various names, in a different business, social science and science domains.

Data analytics on the other hand is a broader term that comprises data analysis as an important subcomponent. Data analytics defines the science behind the analysis; this science means appreciating the cognitive processes used by an analyst to understand challenges and explore data in ways that are meaningful. Analytics also include extraction of data, transformation and loading; the specific techniques, tools and methods; and also how communicate results successfully. Don't forget that data analytics is the process by which we examine data sets in order to draw conclusions about the info they have, increasingly with the help of specialized software and systems and that the technologies and techniques of data analytics are used widely in commercial industries to let organizations make better informed business decisions and by researchers and scientists to either disprove or verify scientific models, hypotheses and theories.

How exactly does data analysis help organizations therefore?

It makes an assessment of the business requirements and looks at how the functions and processes can be used to improve the performance and outcomes. It is done to pinpoint the relevant sets of data and use them to get important insights, which then assist in improving the performance of the business and decision making.

Data analysis aids in breaking down the macro picture into a micro picture to 'dismiss' any sort of human bias with the aid of statistical analysis.

You can use data analysis when your organization wants to make robust business architectures, prepare strong business cases, perform risk assessment, pinpoint market dynamics, gauge the effectiveness of business processes or do an assessment of product performance and so on. When you view historical data, you are able to reveal insights of what worked, what didn't and what is probably expected out of a service and product.

Like I mentioned earlier, it involves professional hands-on exploration of data, drawing up conclusions according to these evaluations, unearthing many different micro views and getting deeper and substantial insights.

Conversely, data analytics assists organizations utilize their data potential to identify fresh opportunities and the entire business to outline the way forward. Data analytics unlocks the right info that a business needs to grow- be it in terms of reducing costs, understanding customer sentiment, improving decision making or even coming with new products and services.

Organizations can use data analytics to measure business results and make changes in business that can bring about better outcomes

By using confirmatory, exploratory or qualitative data analysis, data analytics basically analyzes raw data to derive conclusions to assist make better business decisions.

Data analytics also uses relevant techniques, tools and proficiencies to make an assessment of past performance as well as gain powerful insights about future performance.

Therefore, data analytics is a more exhaustive and very much detailed business practice, which begins with the identification of the kind of data to analyze, then collecting this data and organizing it into the appropriate data sets by use of the correct statistical techniques and algorithms. Data analytics also encompasses a certain amount of data cleaning meant to deliver the right analysis according to which the correct decisions can be made. When this data is converted into a form that is useful, an algorithmic or mechanical process is applied to it in form of statistical process or machine learning algorithm to get insights. You can do this by doing a comparison of the various sets of data to get answers to the problems being solved by the data. When you do that, the data analyst then represents the data in a form that can be properly understood for the benefit of the business.

Data analytics also involves creation of quantitative models by considering the different variables to build predictive models for business opportunities and offer them the opportunities to be able to compete in a heaving marketplace.

In conclusion, we need to get useful information from the 'exponentially increasing' data that is being generated every year- which makes getting useful info from that data increasingly critical.

Alongside data analysis, data mining is a subset of business intelligence, which also encompasses online analytical processing (OLAP), database management systems and data warehousing.

NOTE: As earlier mentioned, all this information is usually stored in a data warehouse, a data repository gathered from different sources, which include corporate databases, summarized info from internal systems and data from the external sources. The data analysis consists of simple query, reporting, more complex 'multidimensional' analysis, statistical analysis and data mining.

Let's now take a look at data mining.

Chapter 4: Data Mining

As you already know, the size of raw data being stored in corporate databases is exploding- the raw data, however, is by itself not providing adequate information. We are living in a fiercely competitive business environment in which businesses have to turn these loads of raw data into substantial insights into their markets and customers in order to guide their investment, marketing and management strategies. This is where data warehouses come in.

Data warehouses

The prices of data storage have generally dropped and this has provided companies with the opportunity to make such an investment a great resource: the data about potential as well as current customers kept in various data warehouses (**see how it works**). The data warehouses are gradually joining the technology. These data warehouses are basically used to unite or consolidate data that is located in different databases. A typical data warehouse will store large volumes of data by particular categories so that one is able to retrieve it more easily, and also interpret and sort it as well. As a manager or executive, a warehouse will enable you to work with many sources of transactional data (or any other data) to respond faster to markets and make business decisions that are more informed. According to projections, every serious business will have a data warehouse in about ten years- but this doesn't mean that just storing data inside data warehouses transforms a company positively. Businesses will want to learn more about the data to grow their knowledge of customers and their markets. It's only when meaningful patterns and trends are derived from the data that the company really benefits.

Data mining

Also known as "discovery of knowledge," data mining is the process of digging through huge sets of data, analyzing them and extracting meaning from that data through computer-assisted methods. The data mining tools predict future trends and behaviors and thus allow business to make decisions that are not only proactive, but knowledge driven as well. The tools of data mining are able to give answers to business questions that would otherwise take too much time to resolve traditionally. These tools essentially scour databases to find predictive information as well as unearth hidden patterns that typical experts may miss due to the fact that it does not lie within what they expect.

'Data mining' is a term that is derived from the likenesses between looking for important information in a massive database as well as mining a hill or a mountain for a vein of precious ore. The two processes do need lots either intelligent probing or intelligently sifting through piles of material to find where real value actually is.

What is the use of mining; what can it really do?

Even though data mining is still young, companies amid a vast range of industries -which include health care, retail, finance, manufacturing, and transportation, aerospace and so on- are using the tools of data mining, and the techniques to utilize historical data. By use of technologies for recognizing patterns coupled with statistical as well as mathematical techniques to be able to sift through the information stored in a warehouse, data mining assists you, the *data analyst* recognize important facts, trends, facts, exceptions, anomalies and patterns that could easily go unnoticed.

Businesses use data mining to find patterns as well as relationships in the data so that it is easier to make decisions that are a lot better. Data mining can help in spotting trends in sales, improve your marketing campaigns and predict customer loyalty accurately. More specifically, data mining has uses, which include the following:

- Market segmentation- data mining will help you pinpoint the common customer characteristics (these are the customers who purchase similar products from your business).
- Customer churn- data mining also helps you predict the customers that have a high likelihood of abandoning your organization for a competitor.
- Fraud detection – data mining will assist you identify the transactions that are very likely to be deceitful or fraudulent.
- Direct marketing- data mining will also help you identify the specific prospects that you should include in a mailing list to get the most response rate.
- Interactive marketing- with data mining, you'll also be able to predict what every person gaining access to a website is most likely interested in viewing.
- Market basket analysis- it will also help you understand the kind of products and services that are usually or commonly bought together- for instance, diapers and beer.
- Trend analysis- it will help you understand the difference between a typical customer the last month and the current month.

The technology of data mining has also been seen to generate fresh business opportunities through the following:

- Automated trend and behavior prediction-this simply means that through data mining, you are able to automate the process of getting predictive info in a large database. The questions that would otherwise have needed extensive practical analysis are now being answered directly from the data. A good example of a predictive challenge is targeted marketing. The data mining technology uses data on promotional mailings from the past to find the target that have a high likelihood of maximizing return on investment in any future mailings. Forecasting bankruptcy and the other default forms, and the identification of a population segment that is likely to respond to particular events similarly are some of the other predictive problems.

- The automated discovery of patterns previously unknown- with the data mining tools, you are also able to sweep through a database and pinpoint the patterns that were previously hidden. A good example of pattern discovery is retail sales data analysis to point out apparent unrelated products that are commonly bought together. The other problems of discovering patterns include detecting fraudulent transactions of credit cards and isolating inconsistent data that is likely to represent keying errors in data entry.

Today, companies use massively parallel computers to dig through data volumes to know about the patterns about their products and customers.

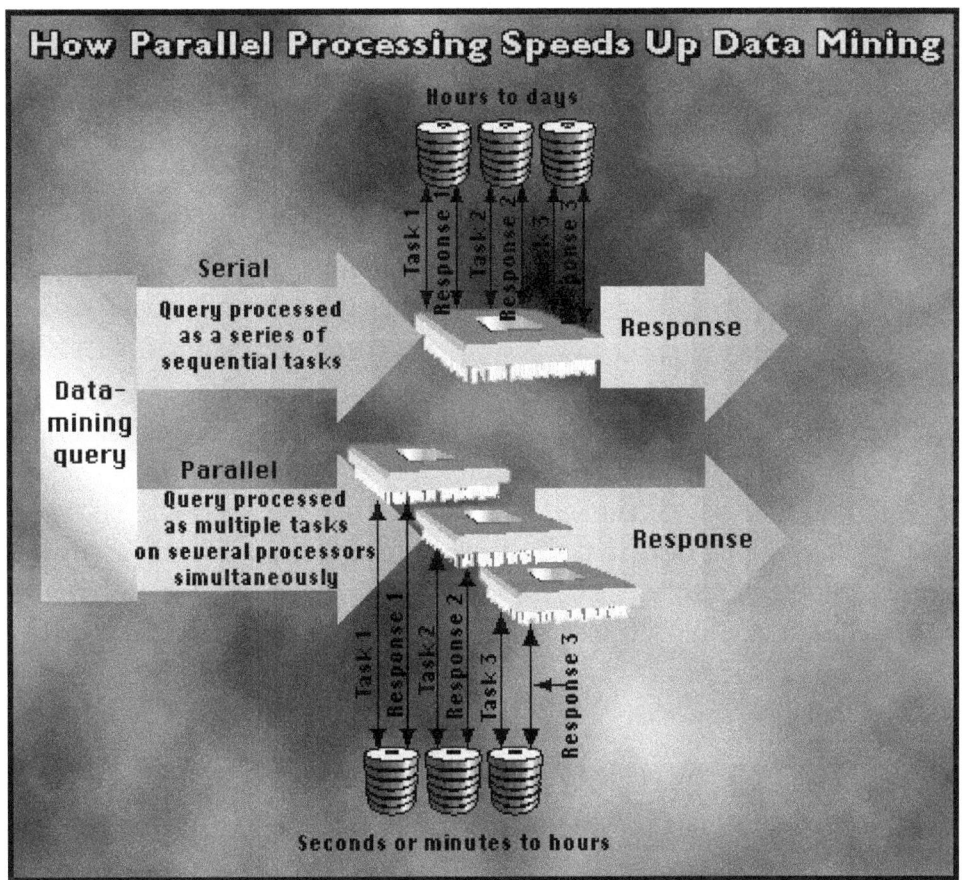

For instance, grocery chains have come to discover that when men enter a supermarket to purchase diapers, they at times tend to grab a pack of beer too. When you have such information therefore, you can be able to lay out the store so that these particular items are closer.

Just to give you a few examples; American Express, A.C Nielson and AT& T are some of the growing ranks of companies that are implementing techniques of data mining for their sales and marketing. These systems are going through terabytes and terabytes of point-of-sale data to assist data analysts understand promotional strategies and consumer behavior- and the reason for doing so is simple: to gain that coveted competitive advantage and of course, increase their profitability.

In the same way, financial analysts are plowing through large sets of data feeds, financial records and other sources of information to make proper investment decisions. The health care organizations are looking at the medical records to make out past trends to be able to cut costs in future.

How data mining works

Have you tried wondering how data mining is able to tell you crucial things you didn't know or things concerning what's going to happen next? I'm sure you have.

The technique that's used to complete these feats is known as modeling. Modelling is simply the process or act of creating a model (mathematical relationship or a set of examples) based on data derived from circumstances in which the answer is known. Modelling techniques have been with us for hundreds of years, of course, but the data storage and communication capabilities needed in collecting and storing large data amounts, and the computational power for automating the modeling techniques to work on the data directly, have been existent only for a short while.

Let's take an example of creating a model. You are a director of marketing for a company dealing in telecommunications. You would like to focus your marketing and sales efforts on population segments that are most likely to become big long distance service users. You know a lot about your customers, but it is not possible to discern the common features or characteristics of your best customers because of the numerous pre-existent variables. From your existing customer database, which has information like credit history, sex, age, occupation, zip code, income, and so on, you can utilize the tools of data mining like neural networks to identify the characteristics of those customers who usually make numerous long distance calls. For example, you might learn that your best customers are the married men between the age of 28 and 37 who earn in excess of $50,000 per year. This then, is your model for the high value customers, and you would thus be able to budget your marketing efforts accordingly.

Perhaps you need a better real-life example:

There is a mail-order business known as Merk-Medco Managed Care that sells drugs to the largest health care providers in the country that include Blue Shield state organizations, Blue Cross, United States corporations, state governments, large HMOs and so on. Merck- Medco is in the process of mining its data warehouse (one terabyte) to unearth the hidden relationship between known illnesses and drug treatments, and then spot trends to assist identify the drugs that are most effective for a particular category of patients. As you would expect, the effect is treatments that are effective and not so costly. The data mining project of Merck-Medco has also assisted customers save about 10-15% on the prescription costs.

In conclusion I can say that in the short-term, data mining results will be in areas of business that are profitable. New niches will be explored by the micro-marketing campaigns then advertising will be geared towards targeting prospective customers with fresh precision.

On the other hand, in the medium term, the truth is that data mining may end up being just as common and simple (to use) as email. We may have to use these tools to get the best airfare to Los Angeles, find a contacts of a long lost childhood friend or find the best prices on dishwashers.

The long-term prospects, as you can imagine, are exciting. Computers could be able to reveal new disease treatments or fresh and different insights into the nature of the universe!

Before we continue, you need to understand that data mining not only depends on computer processing and warehousing, but largely on data collection as well. Therefore, this means that data collection is an important aspect we need to understand. Again, there are some folks who have not been able to properly distinguish between data collection and data mining- while they sound the same, they are actually very different. Let's discuss more on that in the next chapter:

Chapter 5: Data Collection

Unlike data mining, data collection is exactly what it sounds like- the process of gathering and measuring information using software. We currently have many different procedures and techniques of data collection but when we talk about it with regards to big data, we'd most probably be referring to online or electronic data collection.

Data collection refers to the systematic process of gathering followed by measuring information from various sources in order to get a pretty complete as well as accurate picture of a given area of interest. Data collection essentially enables an organization or an individual to answer pertinent questions, assess outcomes and predict on the trends and future probabilities.

Accurate data collection, as you would know, is important when it comes to maintaining the integrity of research, ensuring quality assurance and making informed business decisions. For instance, when it comes to retail sales, data can be collected from website visits, mobile applications, online surveys and loyalty programs to learn more about customers. In a server consolidation project (server consolidation refers to the approach to the effective usage of the resources of the computer server to be able to reduce the total number of server locations or servers required by an organization), data collection would contain an exact account of what each server has installed in it, a physical inventory of the entire list of servers, middleware, the operating system and the app or database supported by the server.

NOTE: the term middleware is just a general term for software that essentially glues together distinct and often complex programs already existing. Some components of software that are usually connected with middleware are web services and enterprise applications.

The Methods Of Data Collection, And Big Data

Collecting information uses a number of primary instruments such as interviews, surveys and focus groups. Currently, with the help from analytics and web tools, your organization can also be able to collect data from website traffic, mobile devices, server activity among other relevant sources of information, of course depending on the project.

Big data describes large amounts of structured, unstructured and semi-structured data that organizations collect. However, it takes a significant amount of time and resources to load big data into a old-fashioned relational database to facilitate analysis, and that is why new approaches for data collection and analysis have emerged. To gather big data and then mine it for information, the raw data with drawn-out metadata is consolidated into a data lake (described below). From here, artificial intelligence programs and machine learning use complex algorithms in the quest for repeatable patterns.

Metadata refers to the data describing other data. 'Meta' is basically a prefix which refers to an underlying description or definition (in most information technology). Meta data makes a summary of the basic information about data, which can make it easier to find and work with specific instances of data.

A data lake in the storage repository which holds lots of raw/unprocessed data in its original/native format until when it is actually required. Whereas a hierarchical data warehouse usually does the job of storing data inside files as well as folders, a data lake usually uses flat architecture to be able to store the data.

The Types of Data

Generally, we have two types of data: qualitative and quantitative data. Qualitative data is any data presented in numerical form such as percentages and statistics. Qualitative data on the other hand is descriptive data- such as smell, appearance, quality and color. Apart from the qualitative and quantitative data, some organizations also use secondary data to assist drive business decisions. Secondary data is normally quantitative in nature and has already been collected for a different purpose by another party. For instance, a company might use data from the United States census to make important marketing decisions. In media, a news team could actually use the health statistics of the government or health studies in order to make decisions regarding content strategy.

With the evolution of technology, data collection has grown and the recent advancements in the internet of things (IoT) and mobile technology are forcing organizations to think about how to analyze, collect and monetize new data. Security issues and privacy issues surrounding data collection are at the same time heating up.

The internet of things is a system of mechanical machines, digital machines, interrelated computing devices, people or animals that are given **special identifiers** *and the capacity to transfer data over a network without the need for human-computer or human-to-human interaction.*

So, how can data collection really assist your organization?

First of all, employing good data collection techniques translates to better decision making. There was a survey that was conducted by **Helical IT** that shows that if a decision is made relying on data as opposed to pure intuition, the chances of being successful are 79% higher. When you implement a data collection process that is centralized, your organization can actually make informed decisions that are driven by data. When a system is already in place, the quantity and quality of data collected by a business over the years, and the manner in which it decides to use it greatly determines not only its competitive advantage but also its sustainability.

Secondly, it means that time at work is saved. According to **Cindi Howson's book** on Business Intelligence, a manager in a typical organization spends approximately 2 hours for each working time block just searching for data. Half of that information unfortunately turns out to be useless later. As a high level manager, when you don't have a data collection process set up specifically for your company, you end up having many wasted or lost hours. A good system will assist gather and display data that is collected from all the different places of your organization if you, the manager, can identify the problems across all aspects of the company easily. You should then display the data collected in a dashboard that is easy to navigate with exact key performance indicators. These KPIs can be presented in charts or graphs with the option of drilling down further to clarify the specific data feeding it.

I believe you are now well acquainted with some of the most common terms around data analytics. In the 17th century, there was an author known as John Dryden who stated that, 'He who would search for pearls must dive below.' While the author didn't say that with advanced analytics in mind, his quote does describe its essence perfectly. We'll now find out how deep you should go into data to get the fact-based insight that is very important.

Side-note: Once your organization begins collecting big data, you should think about getting started on analytics. Unfortunately, not many businesses know much about what this means. Where do you start? What are the types of analytics that would benefit your business the most? Among other important things, let's take a look at the types of big data analytics that you need to consider when you are trying to find the best way to leverage the information in your business.

Chapter 6: Types Of Data Analytics

Descriptive Analytics (What Happened)

This is the most common type of data analytics. It seeks to offer you a comprehensive view of important measures and metrics within your organization. It does an analysis of the data available in real time together with historical data to get meaningful insights concerning the future of the company. The key objective of this type of data analytics is to help find out the various reasons behind past success or failure, which is thus (as a result) referred to as 'reporting bedrock'. It is possible for businesses to learn from their past behaviors though those observations. After that, they can come up with inceptions about their future outcomes.

For example, as a healthcare provider, you will learn how many patients were hospitalized last month; as a retailer, you learn the average sales volume per week; as a manufacturer, you learn about the rate of the products returned for a past month and so on. A good example here would be: as a manufacturer, you are able to decide on the categories of focus products based on revenue analysis, monthly revenue for each product group, income by product group and the aggregate quality of metal parts produced each month.

Descriptive analytics essentially juggles raw data from many different sources of data to offer valuable insights into the past. Nonetheless, these findings tend to signal that something is right or not, without necessarily explaining why. This is the reason why highly data-driven companies are rarely at ease with descriptive analytics alone, and choose to merge it with other types of data analytics.

Diagnostic Analytics (What Made It Occur?)

Next, you have to understand data analytics after having a good understanding of descriptive analytics- this is under diagnostic analytics. Once you assess descriptive data, the wonderful diagnostic analytical tools will enable you, the analyst, to deeply understand the problem with the help drilldowns as well as queries to help you eliminate the root-cause of the problem. In simpler terms, here, historical data is measured against other data to give an answer to the question 'why did it happen?'

Companies are now able to make advances, single out the dependencies and discern patterns with diagnostic analytics. Organizations usually select this type of analytics because it offers them a more profound perception regarding a particular problem. On the other hand, the organizations ought to keep all the comprehensive information by their side, lest the data collection turns out to be time consuming.

Well-integrated and designed business information dashboards assimilating the readings of time series data, and participating filters and drill-down capabilities are considered ideal for this kind of analysis.

Let's take two examples: as a healthcare provider, you compare the response of patients to a promotional campaign in various regions; as a retailer, you drill the sales down to subdivisions.

Predictive Analytics (What's Going To Occur?)

Having the right predictions is important. Predictive analytics involve an analysis of the past patterns of data and trends to forecast the future business outcome accurately. It will help you set very realistic goals for your company as well as its effective execution. You will also be able to moderate expectations, through the manipulation of findings of diagnostic analytics and descriptive analytics.

It is now easy to point out tendencies, exceptions and clusters, while predicting future trends, thanks to predictive analytics; and all of this makes analytics a very valuable tool. When you employ multiple statistical approaches and machine learning algorithms, you are able to predict the possibility of an event occurring in future (with **insight analytics**) - you however need to remember that these assumptions are only based on probabilities and predictions, and thus don't have an absolute accuracy.

Large conglomerates such as Walmart and Amazon leverage this high-in-value kind of analytics to decode trends of future sales, purchase patterns, customer behavior and so much more. Let's take a look in more detail at one company that has used predictive analytics very successfully:

Netflix

Netflix is the most famous internet TV streaming service in the world today and it is being used in more than 130 countries. Now widely considered a global TV brand, Netflix's business model is exceedingly driven by data. The company uses the millions of data bits they have to make predictions of the shows and movies their users would love to watch through their service. The company has loads of data on their watches- which includes the content they watch and how much they watch it, and also demographic data. Netflix then uses this information to make predictions of the kind of content that would be most successful if streamed and what the common or joint success points between them are. The company also uses a well-sophisticated recommendation algorithm to predict what users are most likely desiring to watch.

Again, with the help of predictive analytics and its proactive approach, a telecom company, for example, can be able to identify the subscribers who are very likely to decrease their spend, and thus activate targeted marketing activities for remediation; a management team can also be able to estimate the risks that come with investing in the expansion of the company based on forecasting and cash flow analysis.

Prescriptive Analytics (What To Do)

Prescriptive analytics is where artificial intelligence and big data get into action. Prescriptive analytics is precisely meant to prescribe the kind of action to be taken to deal with the future problem. This follows Predictive Analysis to assist a business understand the core reasons behind complications and come up with the best solution.

It also shares insights on the likely results and outcomes that maximize key business metrics eventually. It works by merging mathematical models, many business rules and data; the data can be internal as well as external and the business rules are preferences, boundaries, best practices among other restraints. The mathematical models include things like natural language processing, machine learning, statistics and operations research (among others).

I admit that prescriptive analytics is complex in nature but when your company uses it, it has a great impact on the overall operations and business growth in future. A very good example of predictive analytics would be a traffic application that makes it possible to select the easiest route to your house, once you've paid attention to the distance of the route, the speed at which you are travelling and the existing traffic constraints. Uber, the taxi hailing company, should undoubtedly rely on this tremendously in recommending routes for its driver-partners and for recommending cars to customers depending on proximity, traffic and other parameters.

Therefore, prescriptive analytics helps to prescribe the kind of action to take in order to eradicate a problem in future or leverage on a favorable trend.

This type of data- usually described as 'state-of-the-art', doesn't just require historical data, but external information as well due to the nature of statistical algorithms. What's more, prescriptive analytics uses sophisticated technologies like algorithms and others mentioned above which make it very sophisticated to manage and implement as well. This is exactly why a company has to compare the efforts needed against an added value it expects before choosing to embrace prescriptive analytics.

The recent trends show that many more companies are beginning to appreciate Big Data solutions and are looking forward to implementing Data Analytics. Nonetheless, it is only that they have to select the right type of analytics solutions to improve ROI (Return on Investment), reduce operational costs and increase the service quality as well.

So what are the types of data analytics companies usually choose?

To know whether there's a prevailing data analytics type, we can turn to current surveys conducted on the topic.

One of the surveys is **big decisions- global data and analytics survey** in which PwC requested more than 2,000 executives to select a category that described the decision making process of their companies best. Further, a questioning was conducted to C-suite on the type of analytics they depend most on. These were the results:

In the category of 'Rarely data-driven decision-making,' diagnostic analytics garnered 58% to dominate the category.

In the category of 'Somewhat data-driven,' diagnostic analytics topped the list with 34%. It was followed closely by descriptive analytics, which had 29% and prescriptive analytics with 28%.

In the category of 'Highly data-driven,' predictive analytics got 36% to lead in the category.

With this survey, we now know that there has to be a need for one or the other type of analytics at different stages of the development of a company. Actually, the companies striving to make informed decisions tend to find descriptive analytics inadequate, and add up diagnostic analytics and sometimes even tend to go further to incorporate predictive analytics.

The same survey also discloses another trend; executives want decision making to be quicker and more sophisticated. What this means is that more businesses will try to enlarge the share of predictive analytics gradually. Another business intelligence trends for 2017 **survey** conducted by BARC confirms this hypothesis. In the survey, 2,800 executives confirmed the increasing need for data mining and predictive analytics.

From the types of data analytics, let's get to one of the most important parts of the book: the process of big data analytics.

Chapter 7: The Process: The Lifecycle Of Big Data Analytics

In the next sections, we'll explore a specific lifecycle of data analytics that organizes and manages the activities and tasks associated with Big Data analysis. Right from a big data adoption and the perspective of planning, you need to note that in addition to the lifecycle, you have to consider issues of training, tooling, education and the recruitment of a team of data analytics.

The lifecycle of big analytics can be divided into the nine stages below.

1. Evaluation of Business Case
2. Identification of data
3. Acquisition and Filtering of data
4. Extraction of data
5. Validation and Cleansing of data
6. Aggregation and Representation of data
7. Data Analysis
8. Data Visualization
9. Analysis Results utilization

Here is an image that represents all the above.

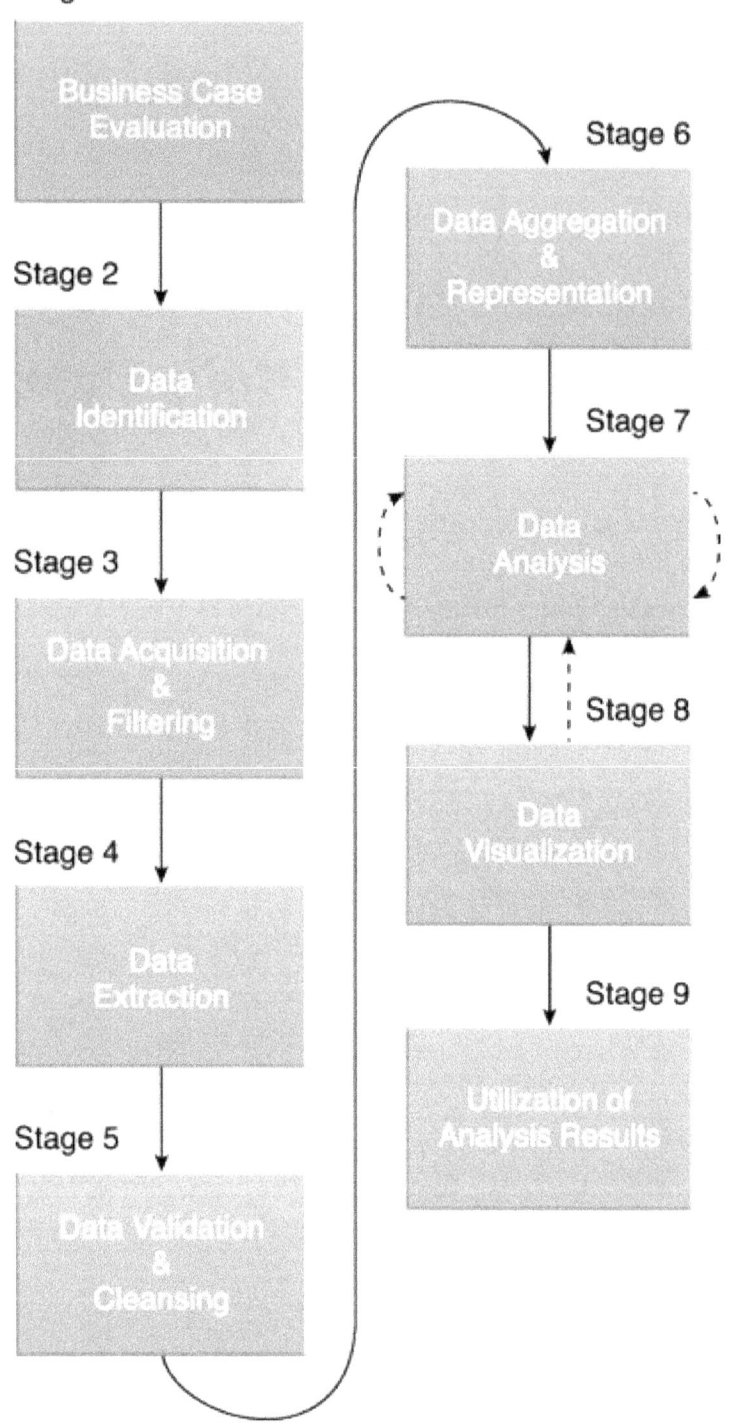

We will discuss this in detail to help you understand what each one of them entails.

1: The Evaluation Of Business Case

Any lifecycle of data analytics should start with a properly defined business case presenting a clear cognizance of the justification, goals and motivation of carrying out the analysis in the first place. The business case evaluation illustrated in the figure below spells out the fact that a business case has to be created, assessed and approved before moving on with the actual practical analysis tasks.

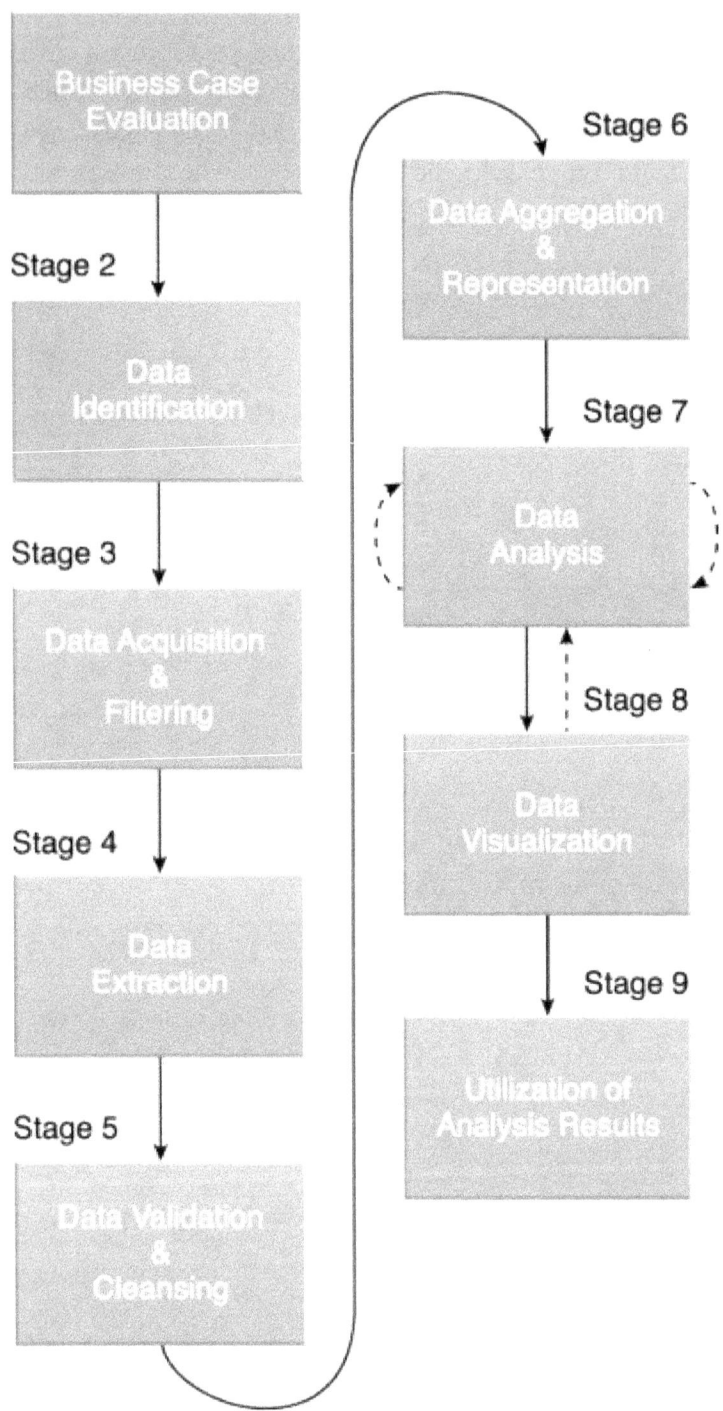

A big data analytics business case evaluation will assist you, the decision maker, to understand the business resources you will require to utilize and the business challenges the analysis will deal with. You also require to go further to identify the KPIs during this stage to assist determine the criteria of conducting assessment and the guidance for the analytics results evaluation. If the KPIs are not presented, you should make an effort to make the analysis project goals specific, measurable, attainable, relevant and timely (SMART).

Considering the business requirements documented in the business case, you can determine whether the business problems that are being addressed are actually problems related to big data. If you want to determine whether a business problem is a big data problem, you have to see that it is related to one or more of the characteristics of big data (velocity, volume, variety) directly.

You also have to note that this stage will produce another outcome: the determination of the basic budget that is needed to conduct the analysis project. You have to understand the needed purchase-like tools, training and hardware in advance so that you weigh the anticipated investment against the benefits of achieving the objectives (that you're expecting). The initial iteration of the lifecycle of big data analytics will need more investment of big data products, training and technologies up-front compared to the later iterations where these previous investments can be leveraged repeatedly.

2: Identification Of Data

The stage of data identification as shown in the figure below is devoted to isolating the datasets needed for the analysis project and their sources.

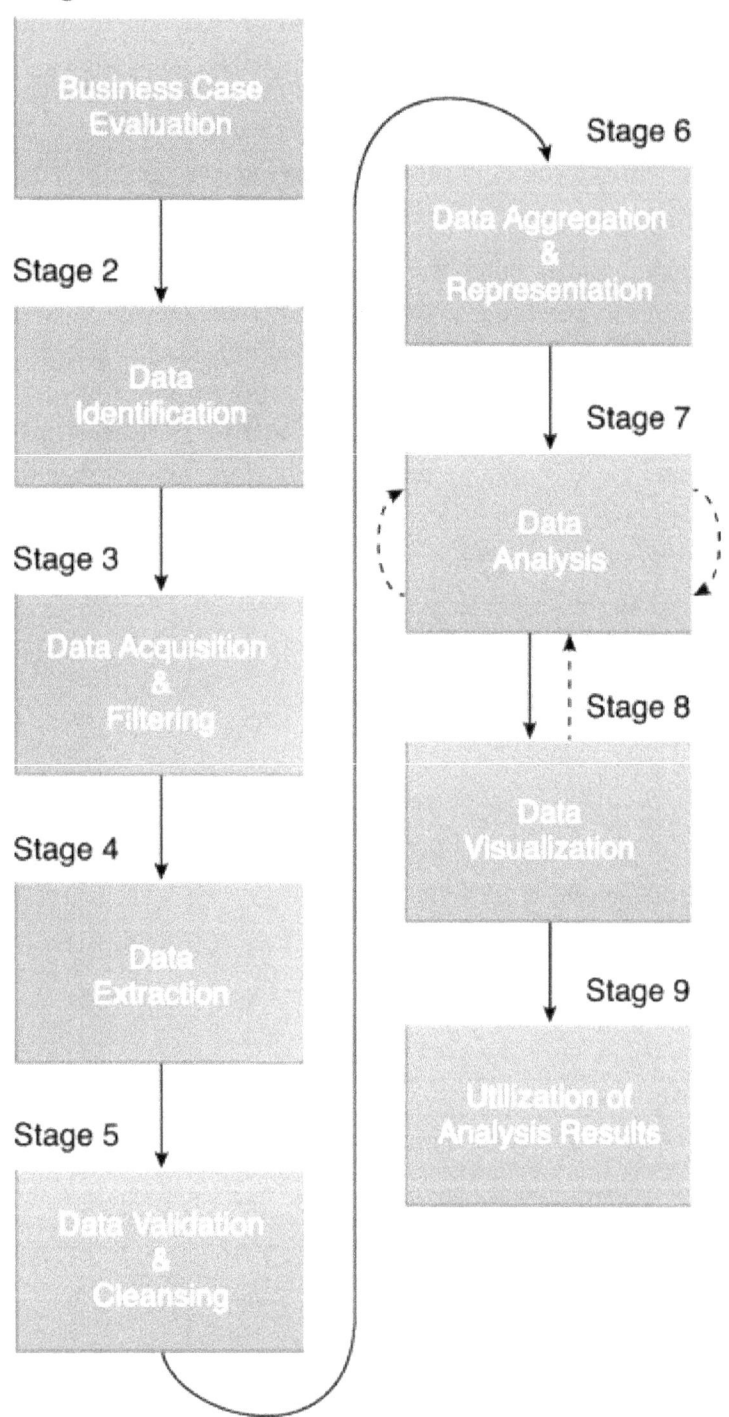

When you identify a wider variety of sources of data, it may grow the probability of discovering hidden correlations and patterns. For instance, to offer insight, it can be helpful to identify as many types of related sources of data as possible, particularly when it is not clear about what to look for exactly. Depending on the scope of the business' analysis project and the nature of the problems in the business that are being addressed, the datasets required and their sources can either be external and/or internal to the enterprise.

If you're dealing with external datasets, you should compile a list of possible third-party data providers such as data marketers and compile the available datasets publicly. You can also embed some forms of external data within blogs or other forms of content-based websites- in this case, you may need to harvest them through automated tools.

3: The Acquisition Of Data, And Filtering

During the stage of data acquisition and filtering as illustrated in the figure below, the data is collected from all the sources of data identified during the last stage. The data acquired is then taken through automated filtering to be able to remove corrupt data, or any data that is considered to have no value to the objectives of the analysis.

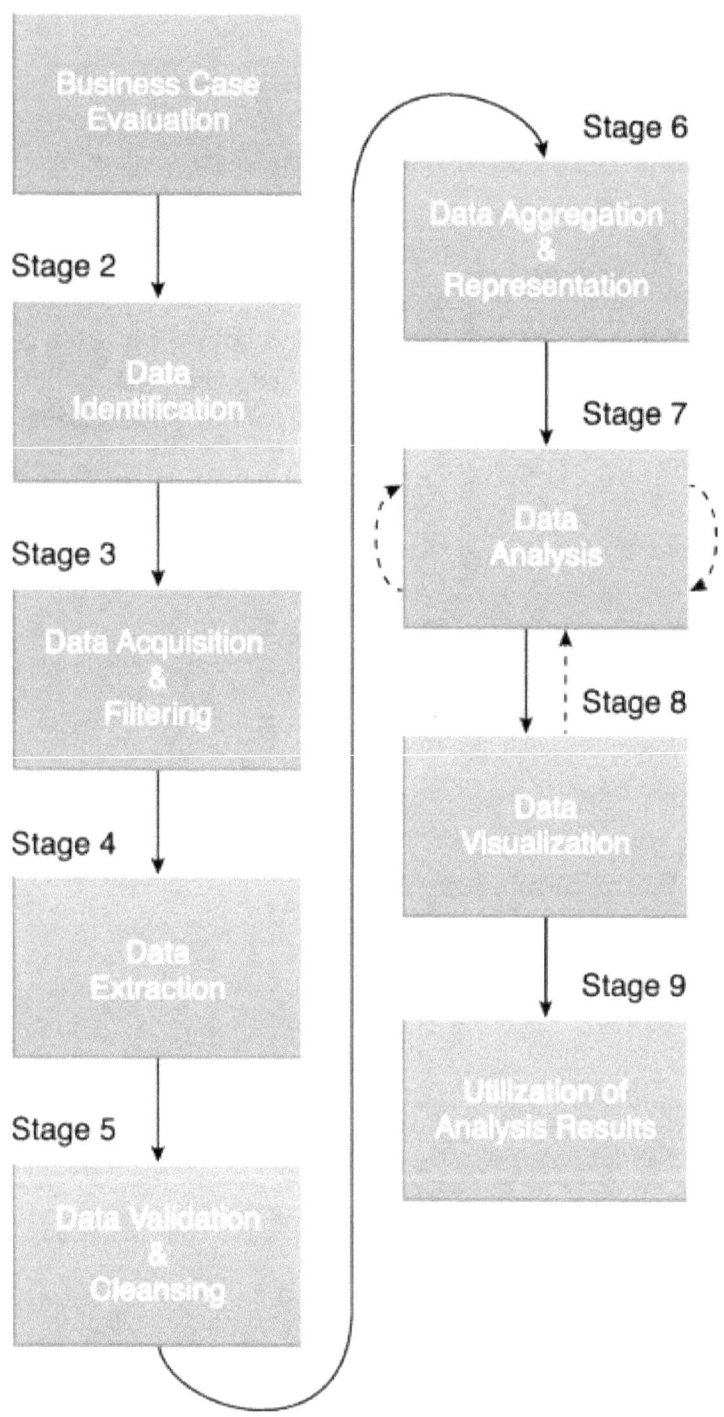

The data, depending on the data source type, may come as a group of files such as data bought from a third party provider, or may need API integration like with Twitter. In most cases, especially with regards to external, unstructured data, some or most of the data acquired may not be relevant and can be cast off as part of the filtering process.

The data that is classified as 'corrupt' can include such things like nonsensical values, records that have missing values or those that have invalid data types. The data filtered out for an analysis may be valuable for various types of data analysis for different reasons. Thus, it is recommended you store an identical copy of the original dataset before you proceed with the filtering. In order to reduce the storage space required, you can compress this verbatim copy.

Both external and internal data has to be persisted after being generated or after it enters the realms of enterprise level. For the batch analysis, this data is supposed to be persisted to disk just before the analysis. If it's a question of real-time analysis, the data is first analyzed before persisting to disk.

As the illustration below shows, you can add metadata through automation from both external and internal sources of data in order to improve the querying and classification. The examples of appended metadata include the structure and size of the dataset, data and time of the creation, source information or the collection and language specific information. It is crucial that the metadata ought to be machine-readable then subsequently passed forward along the subsequent stages of analysis. This assists maintain the provenance of data throughout the lifecycle (of Big Data Analytics) which helps in establishing and preserving the accuracy and quality of the data.

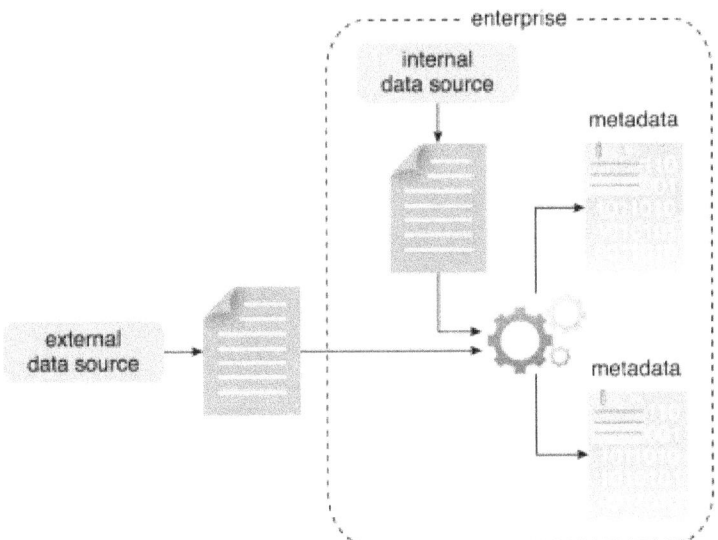

4: The Extraction Of Data

Some of the data recognized as input for the analysis may arrive in a format that is incompatible with the Big Data solution. The need to address distinct data types is more likely with the data from the external sources. You can refer to the data extraction lifecycle stage in the figure below. This is usually meant to extract distinct data and convert it into a format that can be used by the supporting big data solution to help with analysis.

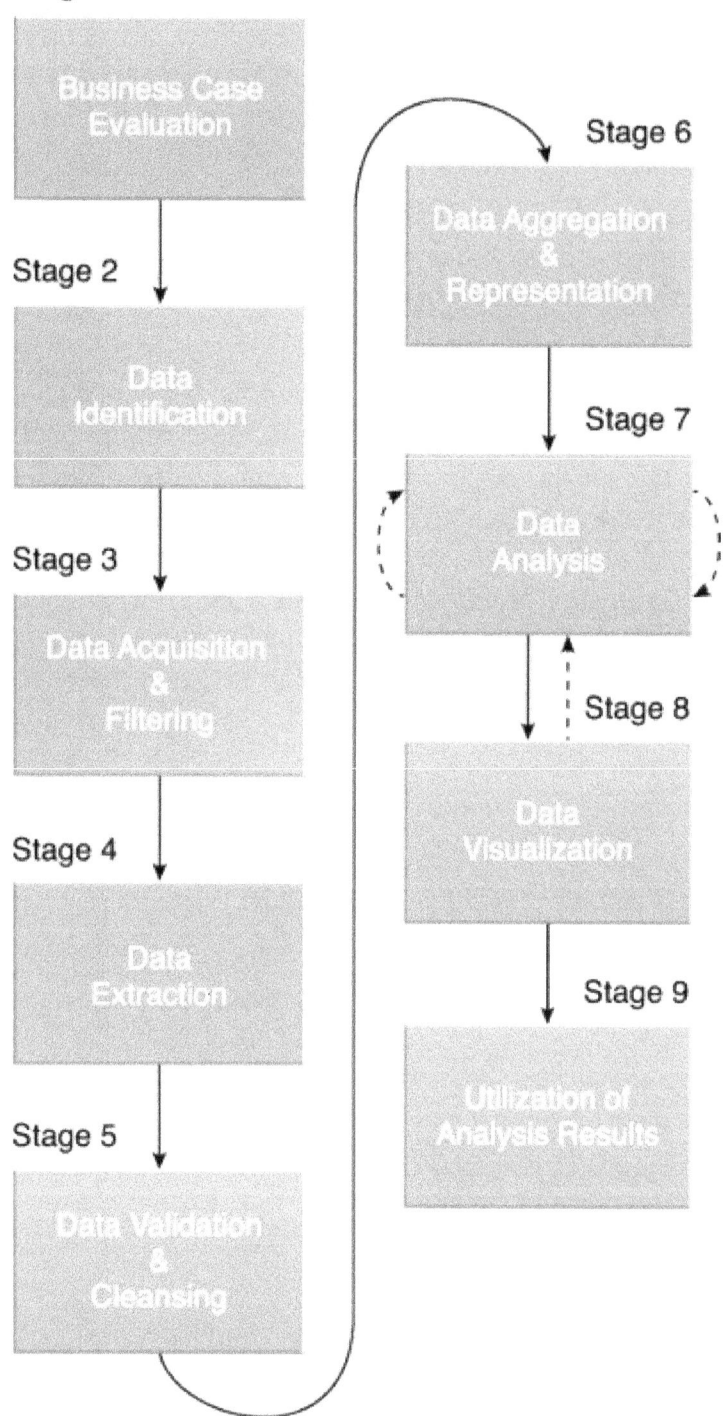

The extent of transformation and extraction needed largely depends on the types of analytics and also the big data solution capabilities. For instance, extracting the fields required from any delimited textual data e.g. webserver log files, might not be so important if the core big data solution can process these files directly.

Likewise, extracting text (in order to perform text analytics) becomes simple if the core big data solution can read the document directly in its native format (note: extracting text to be analyzed basically requires scans of complete documents). The figure below shows comments extraction and an embedded user ID (in an XML document) lacking the need for more transformation.

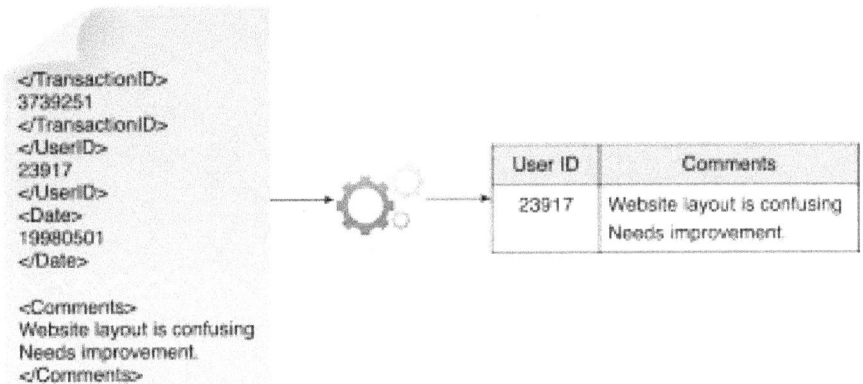

The next figure below illustrates the extraction of the longitude and latitude coordinates of a person from one JSON field.

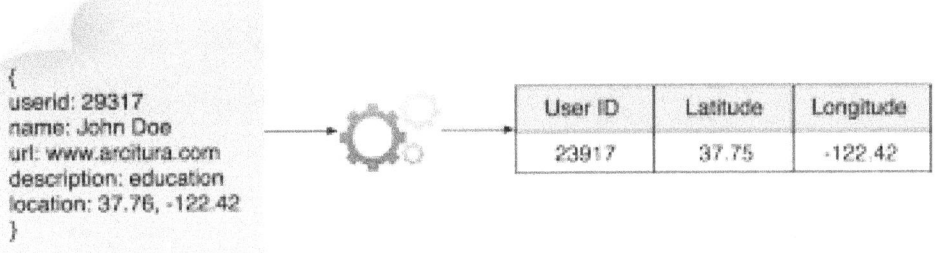

There is more transformation required to be able to separate the data into two distinct fields, as big data solution requires.

5: Validation And Cleansing Of The Data

As you probably know, invalid data can easily skew and falsify the results of the analysis. Unlike the old-fashioned enterprise data, where the structure of the data is pre-defined and the data itself pre-validated, the data input into the various big data analyses can actually be unstructured without validity indication. The complexity it carries can make it more difficult to arrive at a group of appropriate validation constraints.

Below is a pictorial representation of the data cleansing and validation stage.

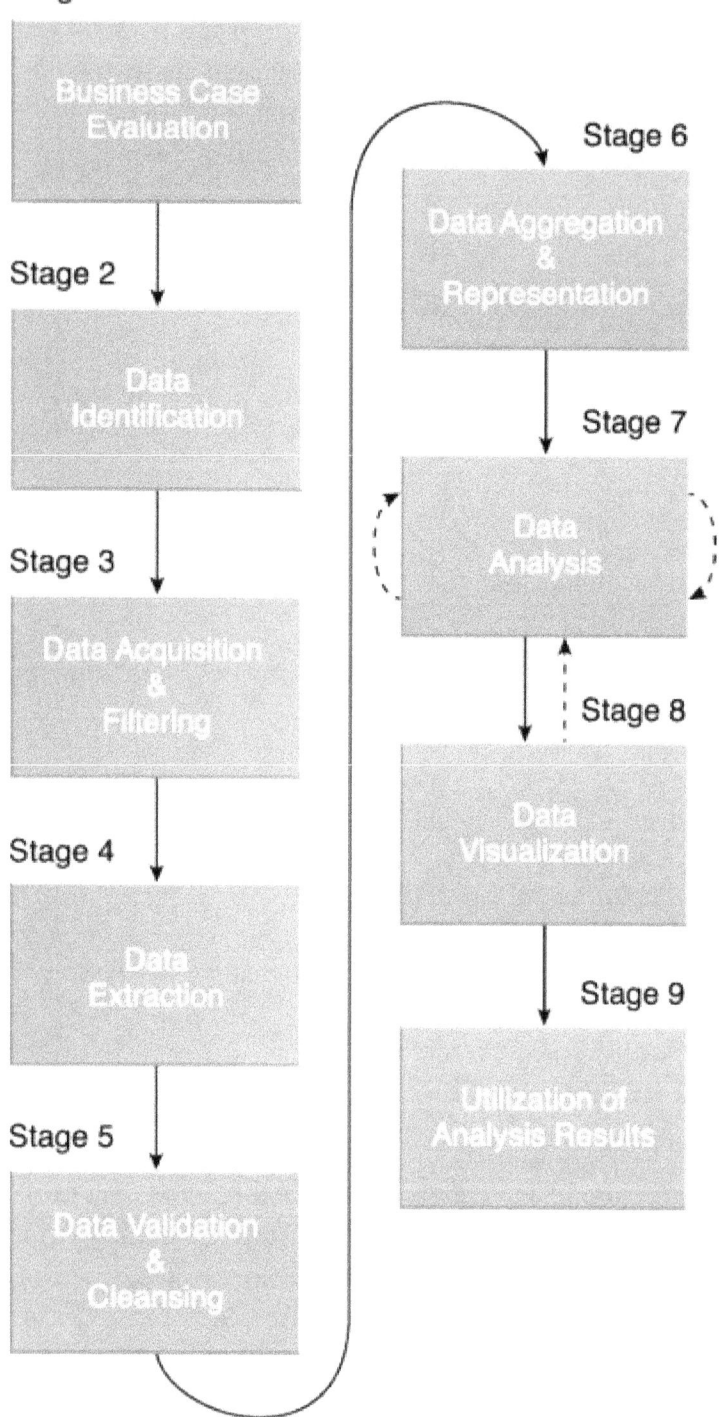

Usually, big data solutions get redundant data across various datasets; and you can exploit this to look into interconnected datasets to be able to bring together validation parameters and fill out the missing valid data.

The figure below is a good example:

- In dataset B, the first value is validated against its matching value in the other dataset (B).
- In dataset B, the second value is not validated against its matching value in A.
- If the value is absent, it's automatically inserted from A.

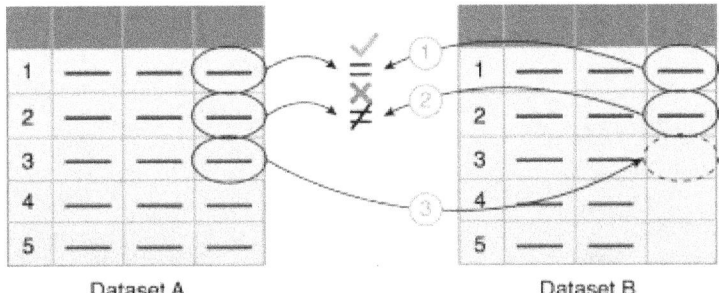

Dataset A   Dataset B

Data cleansing and validation for batch analytics can be done through offline ETL operation. When it comes to real-time analytics, an in-memory system that is more complex is needed to validate and also cleanse the data as it gets in from the source. In determining the quality and accuracy of questionable data, provenance can play a very important role. Data that is seemingly invalid may still be valuable in the sense that it may hold hidden trends and patterns, as the figure below shows.

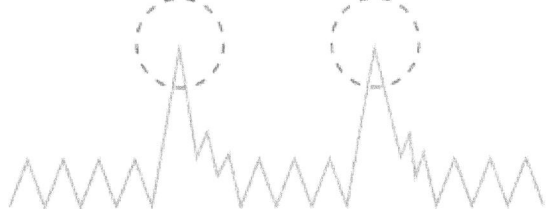

The invalid data results in spikes- but at least it indicates a new pattern, even though it appears abnormal.

6: Aggregation And Representation Of Data

Data may be spread across many datasets, which requires that datasets be linked together through common fields- for instance, ID or date. In other instances, the same data fields may show up in numerous datasets like date of birth. Either way, there is need for a method of data reconciliation or the data representing the right value has to be determined.

The data aggregation as well as representation stage shown below is meant to integrate different datasets in order to have a unified view.

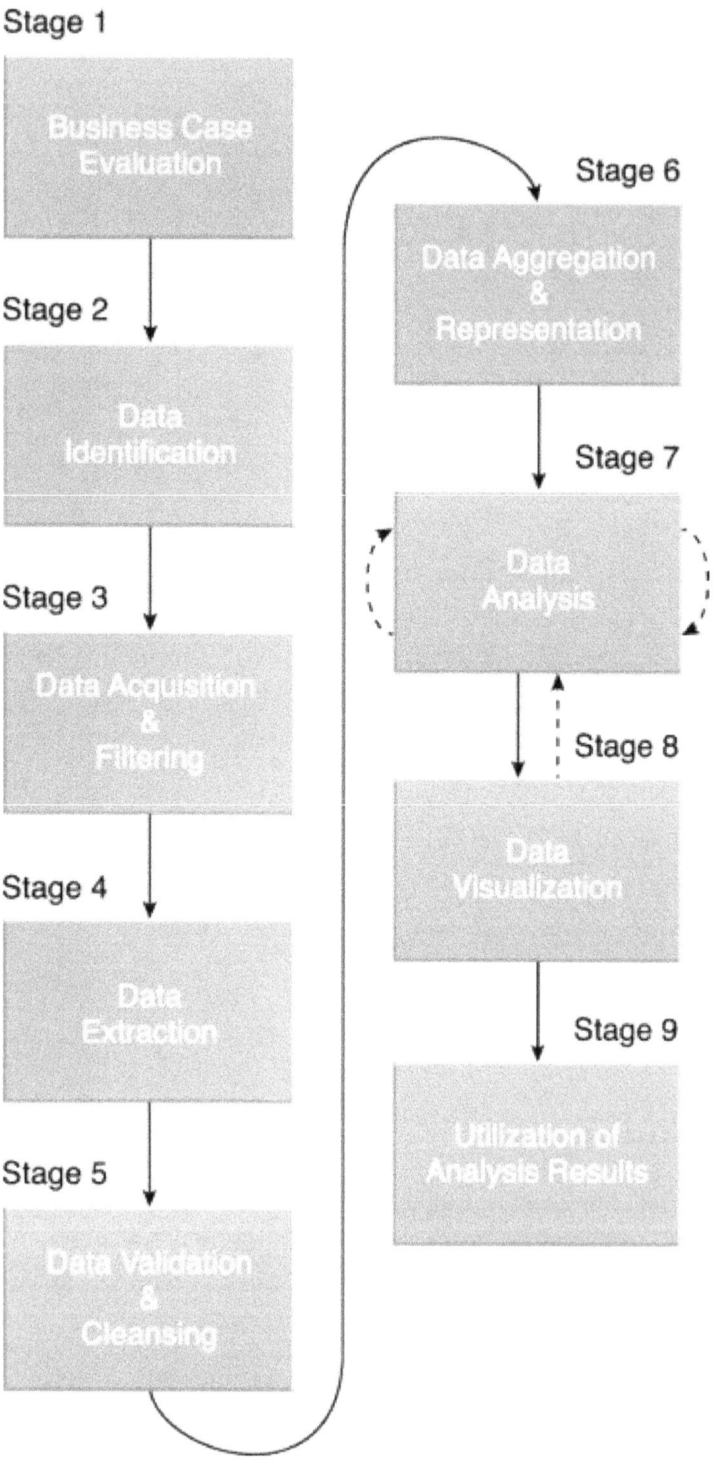

Stage 1

Business Case Evaluation

Stage 2

Data Identification

Stage 3

Data Acquisition & Filtering

Stage 4

Data Extraction

Stage 5

Data Validation & Cleansing

Stage 6

Data Aggregation & Representation

Stage 7

Data Analysis

Stage 8

Data Visualization

Stage 9

Utilization of Analysis Results

Executing this stage can be complicated due to the differences in the following:

Data structure- while the format of the data may be the same, the model of the data may not.

Semantics- a value labeled differently in two different datasets may have the same meaning- for instance 'last name' and 'surname'.

The huge sizes processed by big data solutions can make data aggregation an operation that requires intense time and effort. Reconciling these differences may need complex logic that is automatically executed without requiring human intervention.

The requirements of data analysis in future have to be looked at during this stage to assist foster reusability of data. Whether data aggregation is needed or not, it's important to realize that the same data can be kept in numerous different forms. One form may be better suited for a specific type of analysis than another. For instance, the data stored as a BLOB would have little use if the analysis needs to access individual fields of data.

A data structure that is standardized by the big data solution can assume the role of a common denominator that can be used for many analysis projects and techniques. This may require building a central and standard repository for analysis like a NoSQL database- the figure below describes a good example.

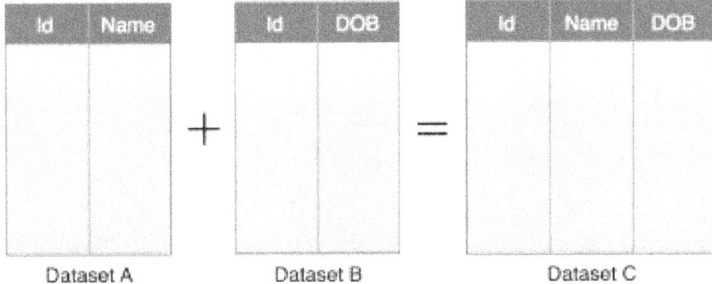

The figure above shows an example of data aggregation in which two datasets are combined or aggregated using the ID field.

The figure below illustrates the same piece of data stored in two different formats. Dataset A has the desired piece of data; but it is part of a BLOB that is unavailable (for access) for querying. The second dataset (B) has the same piece of data organized in storage that is based on columns, which enables each field to have its own querying (individual).

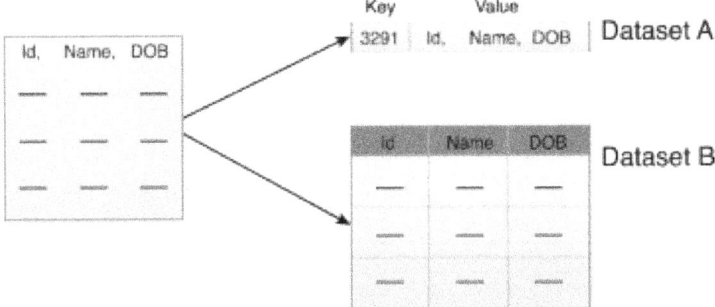

According to the figure above, both datasets A and B can be joined to create a standardized structure of data with a big data solution.

7: Data Analysis

The data analysis illustrated in the figure below is meant to conduct the analysis task itself, which basically involves one or more types of analytics. By nature, this stage may be iterative, particularly if the analysis is exploratory- which would mean that case analysis is repeated until the right correlation or pattern is unearthed. I will explain to you the approach of exploratory analysis in a bit (of course together with the confirmatory analysis).

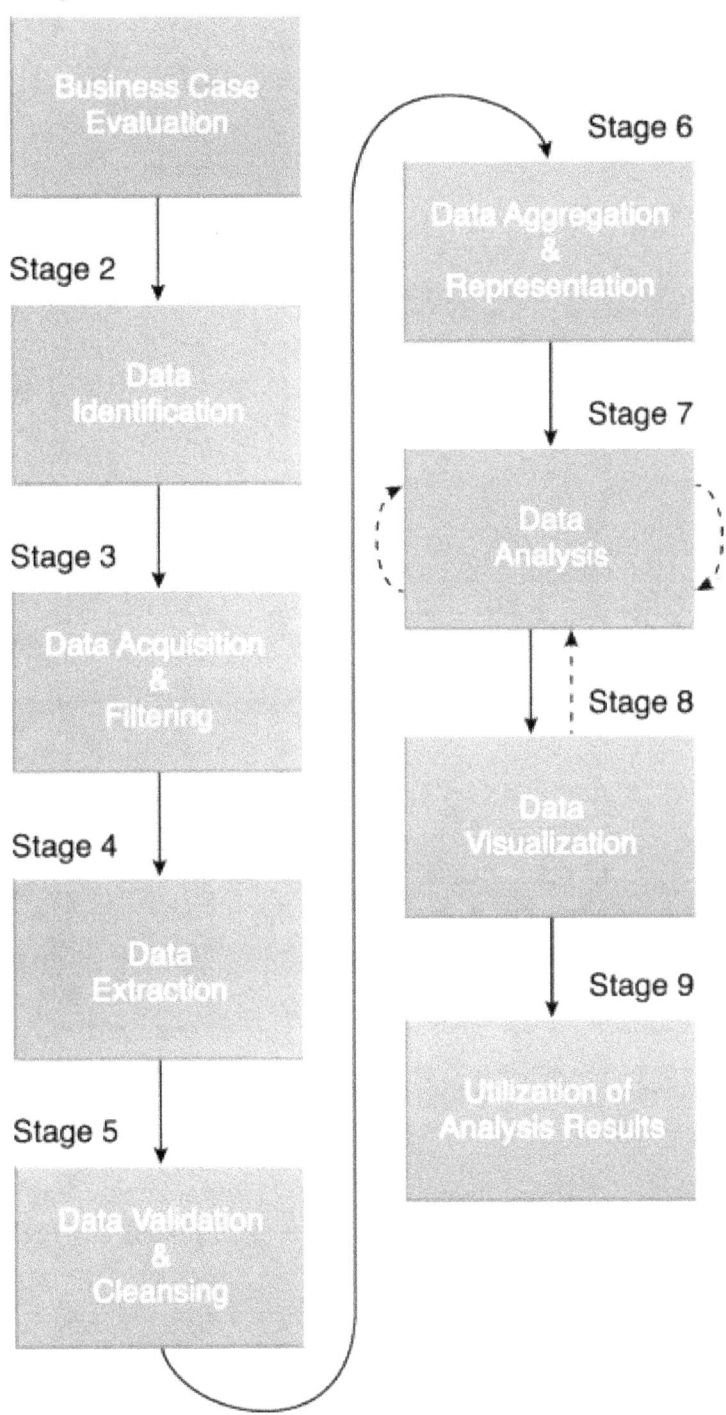

This stage can be as easy as making a query to a dataset to calculate an aggregation for comparison, depending on the kind of analytic end result needed. On the other hand, it may be just as challenging as bringing together the techniques of complex statistical analysis and data mining in order to find out the anomalies and patterns, or to generate a mathematical or statistical model to portray relationships between variables.

Data analysis can be categorized as exploratory analysis or confirmatory analysis, the former of which is related to data mining. See the figure below.

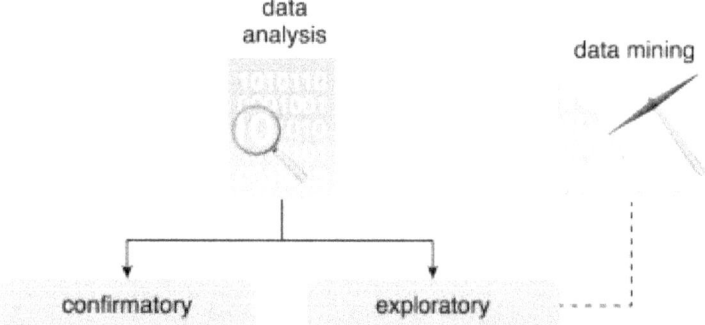

Confirmatory analysis of data is simply the deductive approach in which the cause of the phenomenon under investigation is suggested beforehand. The assumption or proposed cause is known as hypothesis. The data is thereafter analyzed in order to disprove or prove the hypothesis and offer definitive answers to a number of questions. The techniques of data sampling are usually used. Any anomalies or unexpected findings are typically ignored because there was a predetermined cause that was assumed.

On the other hand, exploratory analysis of data is simply an inductive approach associated very closely with data mining. Here, there is no generation of hypothesis or predetermined assumptions. On the contrary, the data goes through an analysis to bring out an understanding of what caused the phenomenon. Even though it may not really bring definitive answers, the method offers an overall direction in which discovery of anomalies or patterns is facilitated.

8: Visualization of Data

The capacity to analyze a massive data amounts to get important insights has very little value if the analysts are the only ones that can interpret the results.

The data visualization stage as shown in the figure below is meant to use tools and techniques of data visualization to communicate the analysis results (graphically) to be interpreted by the business users effectively.

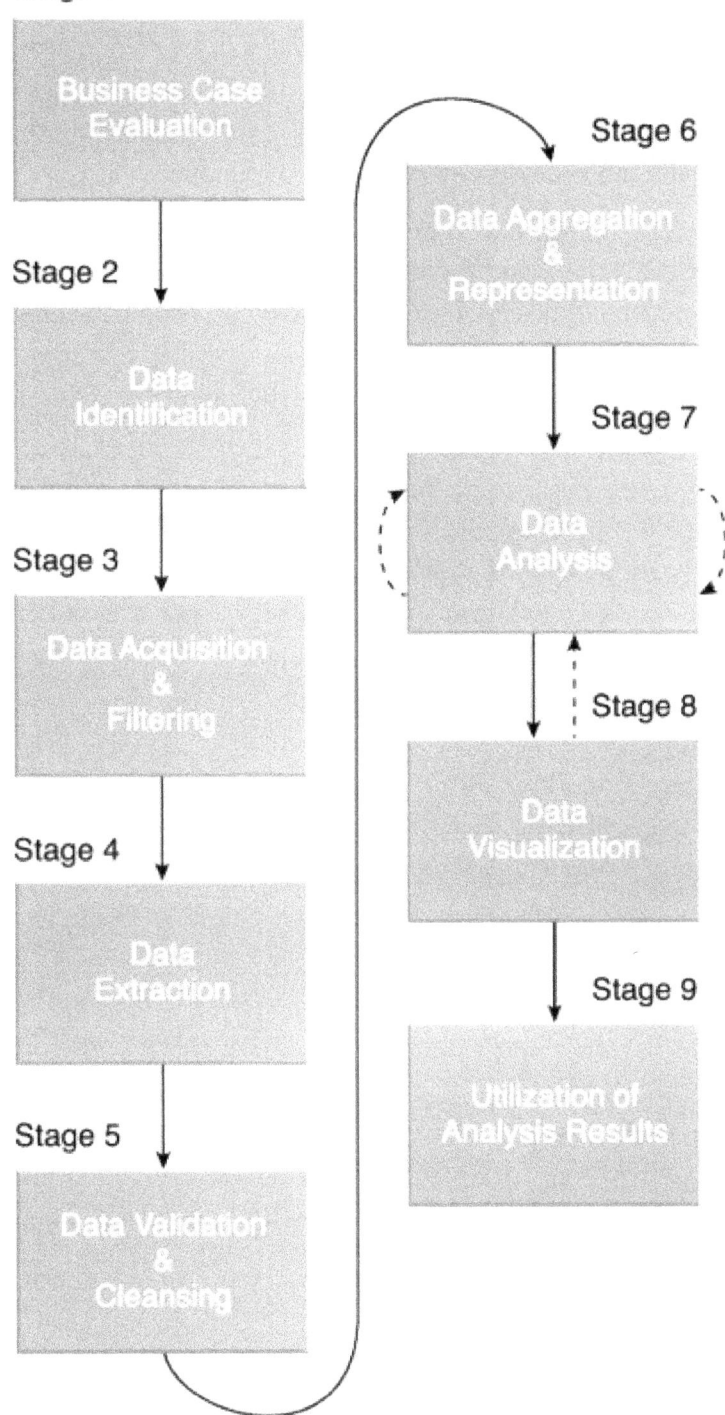

As a business user, you need to be able to understand the results so that you are able to get value from the analysis and in turn have the capacity to provide feedback, as the dashed line leading from the eighth stage back to the seventh indicates.

The results of finishing the stage of data visualization give users the capacity to do a visual analysis, which in turn allows you to discover answers to questions that users have not formulated yet.

These results can be presented in a couple of different ways, and this can influence their interpretation. Therefore, it's important to use the most suitable visualization technique by keeping the domain of the business in context.

You should also keep in mind something else: it is crucial to provide a method of drilling down to relatively simple statistics, so that the users understand how the aggregated or rolled up results were produced.

9: Utilization of the Analysis Results

Following the analysis results being availed to business users to support decision making for business- like through dashboards, there may be more opportunities to take advantage of the results. As shown in the figure below, the utilization of the analysis results is meant to determine how and where the processed analysis data can be leveraged further.

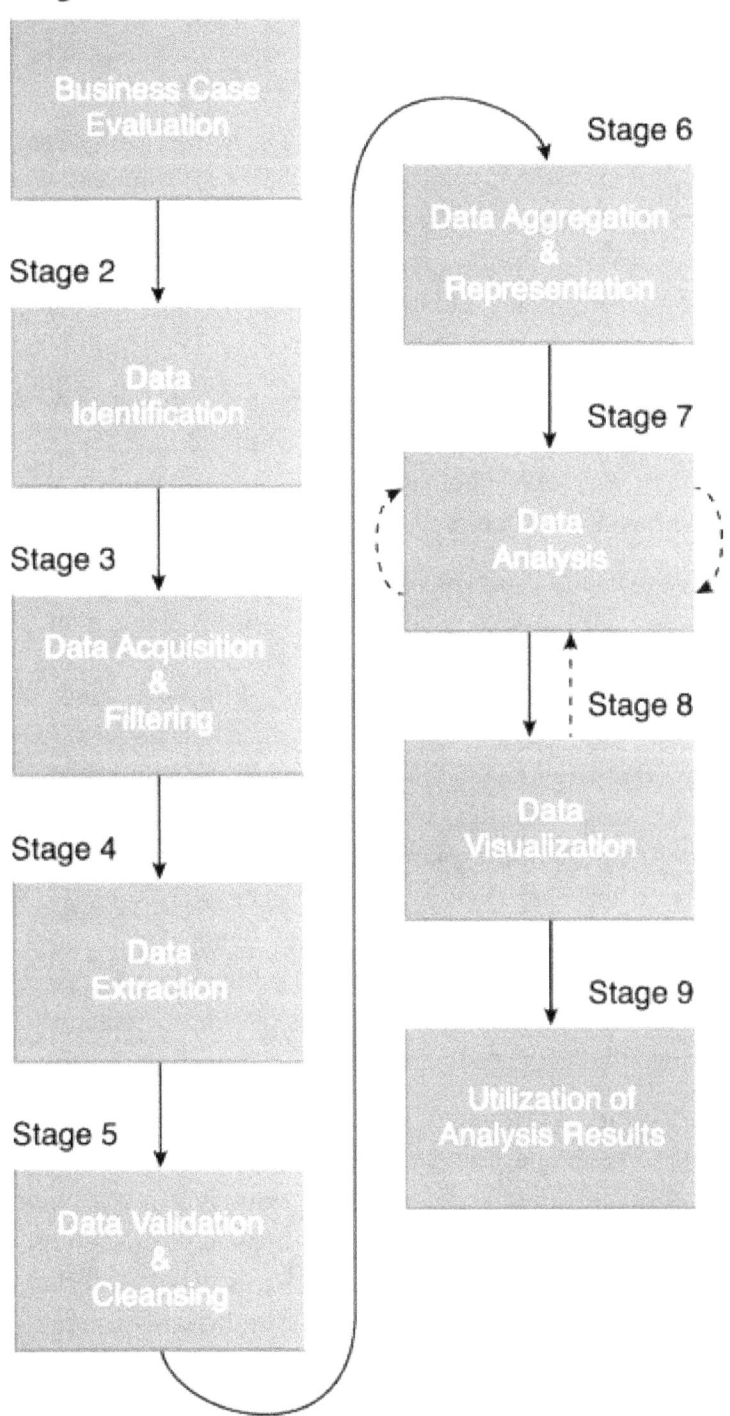

It is possible for the results of the analysis to bear models encapsulating new insights and awareness about the nature of the relationships and patterns existing within the data analyzed- this depends on the nature of the problems of the analysis that are being addressed though. A model may resemble a set of rules or a mathematical equation. You can use the models to advance the application system logic and business process logic, and they can be the basis of a software program or a new system.

During this stage, we have common areas that are usually explored- they include the following:

Enterprise systems input- the results of the data analysis may be fed into the enterprise system directly- either manually or automatically in order to optimize and enhance their performance and behaviors. For instance, you can feed an online store the analysis results related to the customer, which may have an impact on the way it comes up with product recommendations. You may use new models to improve the programming logic within the existing enterprise systems or can become the basis of fresh systems.

Business process orientation- the correlations, anomalies and business patterns found out during the analysis of data are used to hone the business process. A good example can be the consolidation of transportation routes as a part of the supply chain process. The models can also lead to opportunities to advance the logic of the business process.

Alerts- the results of data analysis can also be used as input for prevailing alerts or may become the basis of fresh alerts. For instance, you can create alerts to let users know about an event, which needs them to take a corrective action via SMS text or email.

A case study example

A large part of the IT team of ETIs is convinced that Big Data is the solution or silver bullet that is bound to address all their issues at the moment. Nonetheless, the IT members who are trained point out that adopting Big Data is not the same as just adopting a platform of technology. Instead, a number of factors have to be considered firstly so that Big Data is adopted successfully. Thus, to make sure the impact of factors related to business is fully understood, the IT team has meetings with managers of the business to come up with a feasibility report. When the business personnel are involved at this early stage, it helps create an environment that decreases the gap between the perceived expectations of the management and what IT can really deliver.

There is an understanding that when Big Data is adopted (which is business-oriented), it assists the ETI to reach its goals. The abilities of Big Data to keep and process a lot of unstructured data, and bring together many different datasets will assist ETI understand risk. The company thus hopes that it can reduce loses (as a result) by accepting only the less-risky applicants as customers. Likewise, ETI then predicts that the company's capacity to analyze unstructured behavioral data with respect to a given customer then discover any unusual behavior helps to reduce losses since the company can reject any fraudulent claims.

The decision to have the IT team trained in the Big Data field has improved the readiness of the ETI for embracing Big Data. The team now believes that it has the fundamental skillset that is needed to undertake a Big Data initiative. Data identified and also categorized earlier places the team in a good position to decide on the technologies needed. The significantly early engagement of the management team of the business also offers lots of great insights that allow them to even anticipate any changes that may be needed in future in order to maintain the alignment (with any requirements that are emerging) of the Big Data solution.

At this stage, there's only been a few external data sources identified such as census data and social media. The business personnel have agreed that an adequate budget will be made to acquire the data from third-party providers. In terms of privacy, business owners have shown to be a bit wary- in that getting extra data about customers could easily trigger some distrust from the customers. Nonetheless, it's thought that an introduction of a scheme that is incentive driven like reduced premiums can go a long way to helping gain the trust and consensus of the customers. In light of security issues, the IT team notes that extra effort needs to be put in development to ensure standardized as well as role based access controls are set well for any data that is held in the Big Data solution setting. This is relevant particularly for the open-source database to hold non-relational data.

Even though the business users have depicted excitement about being able to conduct deep analytics by using unstructured data, they pose a question concerning the level to which they can trust the results, since the analysis comprises data from the third party providers. To this, the IT team responds that there will be an adoption of a framework for the addition and updating of metadata for each dataset stored and processed to maintain provenance all the time and so that the processing of results can be traced all the way back to the basic and constituent sources of data.

The present goal of ETI include reducing the time taken to settle claims and detect fraudulent claims. A solution will be required for the achievement of these goals. This is a solution that provides timely results. Nonetheless, it isn't expected that real-time analysis of data support will be needed. According to the IT team, these goals can be easily satisfied when a batch-based Big Data solution leveraging open source big data technology is developed.

The current IT infrastructure of ETI comprises relatively older standards of networking. Likewise, the specifications of most of these servers- like processor speed, disk speed and disk capacity show that they are incapable of offering optimum data processing performance. It is thus agreed that the present IT infrastructural requires to be upgraded before a big data solution can be designed and constructed.

The IT teams as well as the business teams believe quite strongly that a governance framework of big data is needed to help them homogenize the usage of dissimilar sources of data as well as fully complying with any regulations related to data privacy. What's more, owing to the data analysis business focus and to make sure that analysis results that are meaningful are generated, an approach of iterative data analysis in which business personnel from the relevant department are included has to be adopted. For instance, in the scenario of improving customer retention, the sales and marketing team can be incorporated in the process of data analysis right from the datasets selection in order to ensure that attributes that are most relevant to these datasets are selected.

After some time, the business team could offer feedback regarding the applicability and interpretation of the analysis results.

In terms of cloud computing, the IT team takes note that the systems are not hosted in the cloud currently and that the team doesn't have any skillsets related to cloud. These facts, together with the concerns related to data privacy drive the IT team to decide to create an 'on-premise' Big Data solution. As the group notes, there is need for keeping cloud-based hosting open as there is speculation about cloud-hosted software-as-a-service CRM solution replacing their internal CRM System in future.

The big data analytics lifecycle

The big data journey of ETI has reached the stage where its IT team has the necessary skills and the management is well convinced about the potential benefits that a big data solution has to offer to support the business goals. The directors and CEO are very eager to witness Big Data in action. The IT team (together with the business personnel), in response to this, take on the first Big Data project of ETI; the objective is selected as the initial Big Data solution. A step-by-step approach is then followed by the team- this is as laid down by Big Data analytics Lifecycle- in efforts to achieve this objective.

Business case evaluation

Implementation of big data analysis for fraudulent claims detection corresponds directly to a reduction in monetary loss and thus carries complete business backing. Even though fraud takes place across all the four ETI business sectors, the big data analysis scope is limited to fraud identification in the building sector, in the interest of making sure the analysis is somewhat straightforward.

ETI offers building and contents insurance to commercial customers as well as domestic customers. Even though insurance fraud can be organized and opportunistic at the same time, opportunistic fraud in the form of exaggeration and lying covers most of the cases. To measure big data solution's success in regard to detection of fraud, one of the set KPIs (Key Performance Indicators) is the decrease of fraudulent claims by 15 percent.

When the budget is taken into account, the team resolves to focus their biggest expense on procuring of new infrastructure that is suitable for building an environment for Big Data solution. They appreciate that they'll mainly be leveraging open source technologies to support batch processing and thus don't consider that a big initial investment is needed for tooling. Nonetheless, when they put the larger Big Data analytics lifecycle into consideration, they realize that they should budget to acquire extra cleansing and data quality tools and fresher technologies of data visualization. Once these expenses are accounted for, a cost-benefit analysis shows that the big data solution investment can very well return itself a good number of times over if the KPIs for fraud detection can be achieved. Ultimately, the team believes that a robust business case exists because it uses big data for improved data analysis.

Identification Of Data

Some external and internal datasets are identified. Internal data comprises insurance application documents, claim adjuster notes, policy data, incident photographs, emails and center agent notes. External data includes social media data, geographical data, census data and weather reports. Almost all the datasets date to as far back as 5 years. The claim data comprises historical claim data, which in turn comprises different fields where one of them specifies whether the claim was legitimate or fraudulent.

Acquisition And Filtering Of The Data

The policy data is gotten from the policy administration system, claim data and incident photos- the claim adjuster notes are obtained from the claims management system ; the insurance application documents are acquired from the document management system. The claim adjuster notes are presently embedded inside the claim data. Thus, they are extracted using a separate process. The call center agent emails and notes are acquired from the CRM (Customer Relationship Management) system.

The other datasets are received from the third-party data providers and a copy of the original form of the entire datasets is stored in the disk- compressed. The following metadata is tracked in order to seize the pedigree/ or original of each dataset- this includes the name of the dataset, source, checksum, format, size, the acquired date and number of records. A quick data quality check of the weather reports and the Twitter feeds shows that about five percent of the records are corrupt. As a result, two batch filtering jobs are initiated to eradicate the corrupt records.

Data Extraction

The IT team notes that a number of the datasets will require pre-processing to extract the fields required. For instance, JSON format is the format of the tweets dataset. The 'timestamp', 'user id' and the 'text' tweet have to be extracted and transformed into a tabular form so that it becomes possible to analyze the tweets. Moreover, the weather dataset comes in a XML- a format that is hierarchical and the fields like 'temperature forecast', 'snow forecast', 'wind speed forecast' , 'timestamp', 'flood forecast' and 'wind direction forecast' are extracted and kept in form of a table.

Data Validation And Cleansing

In efforts to keep the costs at the minimum, ETI is presently using free versions of the weather and census datasets whose complete accuracy is not guaranteed. Due to this, these datasets have to be validated and also cleansed. Going by the published field info, it is possible for the team to check the extracted fields for any incorrect data or typographical errors- this also includes range validation and data type. As a rule, a record cannot be taken out if it has some significant level of information even though some of its fields may have invalid data.

Aggregation And Representation Of Data

For a good data analysis, it's seen as most prudent to combine claim data, policy data and call agent notes in one tabular dataset in which each field can be referenced through a data query. Apparently, this will not only help with the current task of data analysis, which entails fraudulent claim detection, it will also assist with the other tasks of data analysis like quick settlement of claims and risk evaluation. The resultant dataset is kept in a NoSQL database.

Data Analysis

At this stage, the IT team summons data analysts because the team itself does not have the appropriate skillset to analyze data in support of spotting fraudulent claims. The nature of fraudulent claims first has to be analyzed so that the characteristics that distinguish a fraudulent claim from a legitimate claim are discovered. To do this, the exploratory data analysis approach is used. A range of techniques are applied as part of this specific analysis. This stage is basically repeated multiple times as the results produced after the first pass are not as conclusive as can be to understand what causes a fraudulent claim to be different from a legitimate one. As part of this activity, those attributes that are seen to be less indicative of a fraudulent claim are thrown down and those that carry a straight relationship are added or kept.

Data Visualization

The team has found out a couple of interesting findings and now has to send the results to the underwriters, actuaries and claim adjusters. Different methods of visualization are used; they include scatter plots, and bar/line graphs. The scatter plots are basically used to make an analysis of groups of fraudulent and legitimate claims considering the various factors, such as age of policy, customer age, the claims made and their value.

Utilization Of The Analysis Results

According to the results of the data analysis, the claims settlement and the underwriting users have now developed a comprehension of the nature of fraudulent claims. Nonetheless, in order to achieve concrete benefits from this exercise of data analysis, a model is produced; this model is based on a machine-learning technique, and it is then fused into the prevailing claim processing system in order to flag fraudulent claims.

As we approach the last section of the book, there is something on behavioral analytics I might have mentioned lightly in the previous chapters of this book which I think we ought go into in more detail- this is finding the patterns of customer behaviors. In case you don't know exactly how you can unearth these patterns to make the most of your business, you better pay attention.

Chapter 8: Behavioral Analytics: Using Big Data Analytics To Find Hidden Customer Behavior Patterns

In history, companies have only been able to track some amount of information about their customers like phone numbers, names and previous transactions. We are however now able to track just about every key moment of our lives and turn this info into data.

Businesses can now access a whole slew of fresh info about their customer base across numerous decision points- which include their reactions to various stimuli in advertisements and social media.

Businesses have a great deal of opportunities to understand better how their customers arrive at various decisions as well as predict customers' future behaviors/responses to different stimuli. This means that a customer may not necessarily know how why he bought the jacket, the business from which he bought it will. New, effective techniques enable businesses to actually analyze different data points over a long period of time of interactions so that they disaggregate how customers make their decisions.

As you may know, this influx of data is indeed very exciting, but it is also hard to interpret as well.

Data is meaningless if there is no capacity to interpret it properly, and this is where behavioral analytics comes in. So much like using root-cause analysis to the patterns in weather, human behavior can also be predicted, if the right information is available.

Behavioral analysis targets to understand why and how consumers behave the way they do so that it becomes possible to predict what they'll probably do when they are offered new situations. As a behavioral analyst, when you compile and analyze raw data points like tweets, clicks as well as online purchases, you can be able to uncover all manner of hidden inner drivers. Such important insights will help businesses to understand the approaches to follow in marketing to various customers in different times and places.

Behavioral analytics at work

Currently, many businesses are utilizing these analytics; as an example, there's a company known as Brillio which worked with a US retailer quite recently. The company used behavioral analytics to be able to pinpoint the most loyal sections within their customer base. They tracked millions of people through the years of transactions and were able to make various useful discoveries.

For instance, they learned that customers who engaged with this particular retailer for their wedding planning stayed very devoted to the brand over a significant period of time and became one of the most valuable types of customers they had. The company indeed utilized this insight. They started investing in and marketing towards customers who shared the same underlying traits (particularly during the special occasions) and it brought about a significant revenue uptick and long-standing value.

In another retailer, the company took advantage of a deep learning engine to predict the customer-buying decisions. When customers purchase a pair of shoes or shirt, their brain sort of makes millions of decisions all at once. The company created what's referred to as a neural network algorithm for the retailer to help in modeling the many decisions that take place in the brain when exposed to various forms of stimuli. This algorithm helped the company map the different tastes of customers and they were able to use the map to be able to different future behavior. To give you an illustration, if a customer preferred a specific pair of red shoes, the algorithm would automatically predict their affection for a particular shirt. The company's client used this information to make more effective marketing suggestions that were more targeted.

So, where can you start?

As you already know, sifting through big data is a big undertaking; and even though it does seem like it is too much to process, the good thing is that it can offer a competitive edge to your business. If your business has not yet began harnessing big data analytics to be able to understand customer behavior, it is never too late to begin- just start small but start now.

Find a good partner

I admit that it can be costly and time-consuming to develop this capability in-house. The quickest and safest way to plunge into this space is working with a partner who's got a good grasp of this space and can guide you through it. Just find an established expert who knows your business well and can advise you on how to mine data, and interpret it to generate the kind of insight and impact you require. Even if you choose to work with a partner, you'll eventually need to own this capability. You therefore need to be sure that the journey is strategically building upon your own abilities (this is determined during the phase of generating insights after data analysis).

Answer the right questions

Before you dive in to explore your data, you need to determine the four or three big questions, which need to be answered first. This is important because it is usually easy to let new seemingly exciting paths to distract you when you begin to look at the data.

The sample questions can be: who are my favorite customers? How do these customers shop?

When you narrow this down, you will get a clear focus which will assist you guide the data ecosystem you want to define.

Make it sustainable

When you begin using data to find the answers to these questions, you might want to consider how the answers can change over time. As you create your data ecosystem, you can try to describe a process that can be refreshed and recreated. This way, you'll be able to respond to the same critical questions in future and also be able to answer new questions coming up along the way as well.

For instance, when you embark in a major data processing before a project, you need to ask your teams to record these steps and also keep all the links and sources live. This allows your data engineering team or partner to execute refreshes in future when there is a generation of new data. This agility prepares you to manage changes as they occur.

Do not wait until the data is faultless

Last but not least, this is the worst time to be a perfectionist- there are analyses that could take several years to get right. Executives usually delay on making decisions that are based on data until the analysis is completely correct. This can waste valuable resources and time. Instead of just waiting for an entirely clear result, you need to pay attention to what signals your data is having and know you are making decisions with a particular level of confidence (which is in most cases enough to make a no-go/go decision).

In this case, don't forget that it is often riskier not to take risks. If you are ready and willing to fail quickly, small and cheaply, your company will learn and as a result, become stronger and wiser. For forward thinking folks, big data can bring about larger profits. You thus need to partner with the best tools and people you can get and dive in!

One real example:

Capital One

This company has, for a long time, been relying on behavioral data in order to shape its offerings to various customers. For example, their deal optimization engine helps to analyze demographics as well as spending patterns of customers to determine when, where and how to place offers before people- this leads to increased revenue for the company and a better experience with the brand for the customers. They have also created a tech driven think tank called Capital One Labs in which employees sort through prospective opportunities such as new modes of banking using big data.

As you ruminate on behavioral analytics, you need to consider something else that is equally important to note: the need for a more advanced approach to big data to help with pattern discovery, among other things.

In the recent years, companies have increasingly become engrossed on how to store and manage big data. How should they architect their enterprise stack best- to gain value from Big Data in terms of Hadoop, NoSQL, traditional data warehousing and complex event processing? Should they host our data on the cloud or on-premise? In as much as these are fair questions to ask, they don't actually get to the center of why Big Data is so much of a big deal as we tend to put it. It is only by using advanced analytics i.e. using machine learning to be more specific, can organizations be able to tap into their abundant experience vein truly, and mine it to discover insights automatically and generate pretty predictive models so as to utilize the entire data that they are capturing. With this technology, instead of looking into the past for producing reports, your business can be able to predict what will happen in future by analyzing the existing data.

Let's talk more about that in the next chapter:

Chapter 9: Further Pattern Discovery In Advanced Analytics: Machine Learning

To put it simply, the value of machine learning is rooted in its capacity to accurately create models to guide actions in future and discover patterns that have never been seen before.

There is a great deal of confusion about the real meaning of machine learning with regards to Big Data. Along with predictive analytics, prescriptive analytics and deep learning, many vendors of software claim they conduct machine learning. It's important to know what these terms mean so that purchasers as well as vendors know what to expect from a particular software solution and where its value is.

Machine learning is basically the modern science of getting patterns and generating predictions from data based on the work in data mining, multivariate statistics, pattern recognition and advanced analytics. The methods of machine learning are especially effective in situations where predictive and deep insights have to be unearthed from large, diverse and quick-changing datasets. Across these data types, machine learning outperforms the traditional methods quite easily on scale, speed and accuracy. For instance, when doing fraud detection within the short period of time it takes to swipe a credit card, you can rely on machine learning to rule on the information that is linked with the transaction (like location and value) as well as leveraging historical data and data about social networks for the correct assessment of potential fraud.

The methods of machine learning are vastly superior in making analyses of potential customer mix across data from many different sources like CRM sources, transactional sources as well as social media. High performance machine learning could actually make an analysis of the entire big data set as opposed to a sample of it. This scalability enables predictive solutions based on complex algorithms to be a bit more accurate, and also pushes the importance of the speed of the software to construe the billions of columns and rows in real time, and also in analyzing live streaming data.

If you get to practice and develop the technology of machine learning, you'll realize that it's no longer enough to provide the capacity to achieve fast, scalable predictive and the most accurate insights. In the end, for machine learning to have a positive impact in our world, we have to deliver it (machine learning) in a more usable and smarter form.

Methods of machine learning

In machine learning, there are many methods used but the most popularly adopted are supervised and unsupervised learning. Let me describe these briefly.

Supervised learning

Here, algorithms are trained by use of labeled examples like input where the wanted output is known. For instance, some equipment could have points of data labeled either R (runs) or F (failed). The learning algorithm gets a set of inputs together with the corresponding correct outputs; the algorithm learns through a comparison of its actual output with the right inputs to get errors. After that, it modifies the model consequently. Supervised learning, through regression, classification, gradient boosting and other methods, uses patterns to make predictions of values of the label on extra unlabeled data. Supervised learning is usually used in applications where the future events are predicted using historical data. For instance, it can 'predict' when different transactions of credit cards might be fraudulent, or the insurance customer who has a high likelihood of making a claim.

Unsupervised learning

This one is used with respect to data, which does not have any historical labels. In this case, the system is not given the 'correct answer'. Instead, the algorithm has to make out what's being displayed. The goal here is to explore the data and find a structure inside. Unsupervised learning operates perfectly on transactional data. For instance, it can pinpoint customer segments with the same qualities that separate segments of customers from each other. The popular strategies include k-means clustering, nearest-neighbor mapping, singular value decomposition as well as self-organizing maps. These algorithms also tend to be used in segmenting segment text topics, identifying data outliers as well as recommending various items.

The following steps describe how to apply machine learning to improve your analytics:

Learn the science

You need to learn the science behind machine learning, including what it can do with data and what it can't. For instance, do you know the methods of machine learning and what they mean? Even a bit of knowledge will go a long way towards assisting you identify the opportunities and consultants for analysis.

Begin with basic connectivity and collection of data

The journey to machine learning and advanced analytics begins with data collection and basic connectivity. This journey entails pinpointing the different questions, which can best be answered through data analysis coupled with identifying the data, which would be needed to answer those questions and then setting up the right processes to help gather the right type as well as amount of data to support machine learning properly.

Have a clear goal

You need to make sure you have a clear goal for the analytics. Train the machine. You have to ensure you have the data and a good understanding of what the machine should learn, or its success might be unattainable. Nonetheless, that does not mean that you need to have a fully comprehensive plan either. The best project result may be that the analytics might have a positive surprise.

Begin with an internal project

Now look for an interesting problem that the team desires to crack, and let them develop their machine learning skills while working on a problem that they are passionate about.

Hire an expert

Next, look for a skilled data scientist who can work with the business sponsor and tech department. For the first project, select a little, 'low-hanging fruit' that can depict true business value. Select a project in which there is enough amounts of data and a well-defined result which can be demonstrated. The applicability of the data can be validated by the data scientist.

Before you sprint, learn to crawl and walk

Big data does not always necessarily mean zettabytes, but that more data is always better than more complex algorithms. If you are to use machine learning to improve analytics, you need to try to crawl first; this means collecting all data in a set/batch for a full historical analysis. In order to walk- you first have to move into real-time collection and also descriptive analysis. In order to sprint, you ought to use the same real-time framework for collection for predictive analytics as well as prescriptive analytics.

Test the tools for free

At this point, you can now get your hands on a number of actual technologies or products to test. Through both Azure and AWS, you can get some free time to survey the tools of machine learning for data analytics by visiting sites like **this one**. By viewing the technologies that are out there, you'll definitely learn more and be able to see the potential for your own business.

Look for cloud solutions

We currently have complex machine learning algorithms available on demand through the cloud. For a tech department, the first step is to start the process of integrating with cognitive computing, application development capabilities and data science to enable organizations to merge structured data with unstructured data, external data for the automation of the process of analytics –which would otherwise consume too much time.

Begin with a single project

You should not try applying machine learning to each and every data problem you have at the same time as it will become too overwhelming too soon. Begin with one familiar data analytics project and see whether machine learning yields results that are comparable to those you would expect. When you now know that machine learning is assisting you achieve your goals, advance to the next project. It is important to make one step at a time.

Ensure there are quality data and processes

You need to ensure you've got the best data possible. Start by cleaning up your database; ensure your sources of data are feeding you quality data; set standards of data governance and train your team members on the relevance of top-quality data. You have to begin with the finest information on which to model so that you get the most out of this machine learning technology - in any case, machines are only as good as the info you feed them.

Answer specific questions

Tech departments tend to approach machine learning in more or less the same way as a science project, in which the objective is to solve all the pieces of the puzzle at once. Indeed, there are very many questions they can ask but it is important to determine the exact parameters that will bring them the quickest value and keep answering specific questions in order of priority. This approach naturally solves the bigger problems over time.

Let's now take an example of where machine learning is used today:

Pinterest (for improved content discovery)

It doesn't matter whether you have never used the site before, or you are a hardcore pinner, Pinterest takes a curious place in the ecosystem of social media. Since the primary function of Pinterest is to curate current content, it only makes sense to invest in technologies that can make this process more effective as a priority- which is the case at Pinterest.

Back in 2015, Pinterest adopted Kosei, a machine learning company specializing in the machine learning tech commercial applications (content discovery and recommended algorithms to be precise). Today, machine learning is touching just about every aspect of the business operations of Pinterest –right from spam moderation and content discovery to advertising monetization; actually, it also helps in decreasing the churn of email newsletter subscribers. How cool is that!

Edgecase (to improve E-commerce conversion rates)

For many years now, retailers have been struggling to overcome the huge disconnect between shopping online and shopping in stores. For the whole talk about the way online retail will turn out to be the death-knell of old-fashioned shopping, most E-commerce sites are still not very appealing.

Edgecase, which was formerly called Compare metrics looks to change that.

With the machine learning technology it is using, Edgecase hopes it can assist e-commerce retailers improve user-experience. Besides streamlining the e-commerce experience to be able to improve conversion rates, Edgecase is planning to leverage its tech to offer shoppers (who may not have a clear idea of what they are searching for) a better experience, by analyzing particular actions and behaviors which show commercial intent- this is an attempt to make casual online browsing more fulfilling and closer to the old-fashioned retail experience.

Conclusion

We have come to the end of the book. Thank you for reading and congratulations for reading until the end.

Data analytics is a broad concept, as you have seen, that encompasses many other valuable concepts. We have discussed some of the most important things regarding data mining, Big Data analytics, data collection, Business intelligence, the concepts related to it and so much more. In each concept and chapter, we could not have exhausted everything; you thus need to do more research on each one of them to gain a deeper understanding.

I am however glad you have read the book up to this point because it means you are more informed about data analytics- it's importance, and how to conduct it for the growth of your business.

If you found the book valuable, can you recommend it to others? One way to do that is to post a review on Amazon.

Part 2: Data Mining

The Data Mining Guide for Beginners, Including Applications for Business, Data Mining Techniques, Concepts, and More

Introduction

Data mining refers to the process of cleaning, collecting, processing, analyzing, and extracting important information from data. There exists a big difference based on the domain of the problem, formulations, applications, and data representations. In other words, data mining is a wide term that describes different aspects of the data processing.

In modern times, each automated device and system produces some form of data, which can be for analysis or diagnostic. This has created an entire repository of data. This data repository is because of the advancement in technology and the computerization. It is now vital to determine whether it is possible to mine accurate and actionable insights from existing data. This is the time when data mining becomes critical. Usually, the raw data is unstructured and in a format which is not desirable for automation. For instance, data that has been collected manually could be extracted from heterogeneous sources in different forms, but it requires processing using a computer program.

From an analytical point, data mining is not easy. It is difficult because of the broad differences in the data types. For instance, an intrusion detection system is different from a commercial product problem. Still, within the same classes of problems, the differences are obvious.

In this book, each chapter will educate you on the major concepts in data mining so that you can prepare yourself to master data mining techniques.

Chapter 1: Overview of Data Mining

The potential of data mining is an inspiration to most top organizations. Data mining is defined as the extraction of information produced at different times in our lives. When we work with data, we start to discover the benefits of finding patterns and their actual meaning.

The modern sector is driven by data. Corporate data together with the customers' data has been identified in all spheres of life as an important asset. Decisions that depend on objective measurements are better than those defined on subjective opinions that could turn out to be wrong. Data is collected from different devices and has to be analyzed. Once it has been analyzed, it is processed before converted into information.

Some of the devices used to accept data include data loggers, cashiers, Enterprise Resource Planning, and warehouse audits. The ability to mine hidden but useful information from data has become critical in the modern world. When data is used in prediction, it makes the future characteristics of a business to be clear. That plays a big role in the business sector.

As you can see in the figure below, the importance of historical data can result in a predictive model, and a means by which one can hire new applicants in the business scheme.

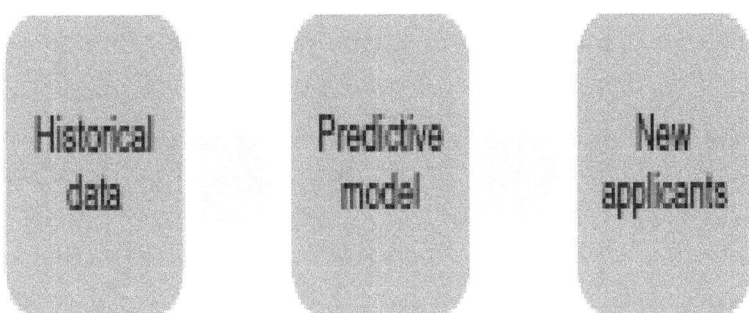

With the emergence of developments in the technological industry, there has been a huge growth in the hardware and software industries. Complex databases have been developed which have helped to store large data sets. This has brought up the need to mine data in different environments. The different contexts include data collection, machine learning, description, prediction, and analysis.

Nowadays, many people are interested in intelligence, and they need to make sense of the massive terabytes of data stored in the databases and develop important patterns from it.

Data mining is a great process that a lot of different companies are going to employ. It is a process that allows a business to turn their raw data into useful information. With the help of some specialized software, the company is able to take a large batch of data and then look through it to find patterns. With the information that is gathered, the business is able to learn more about their customers and can develop more effective marketing strategies to decrease cost and increase sales. Data mining is going to depend on the business being able to effectively collect the data, proper warehousing, and computer processing.

A good example of a type of business that uses data mining techniques would be grocery stores. Many supermarkets like to offer some loyalty cards to customers so that these customers can receive reduced prices that are not available to other shoppers. The customer gets the benefit of saving money, and the business gets an easy way to track who is buying what, when they are making the purchase, and how much they are spending.

The grocery stores are then able to take this data and can analyze it for several different purposes. They may offer their customers coupons that are targeted to the customers' buying habits or they can use it to help them decide which items they want to offer for sale and which ones will be offered at full price.

There are a lot of good information that a company can gather from this information, but it can be a cause for concern when the wrong information, or the information that is not representative of the overall sample group, is used to form the hypothesis. This can lead the business astray and can make it hard for them to reach the target market that they want.

When companies decide to centralize all the data that they collect into one program or database, they are going through a process known as data warehousing. With this, a company may spin-off parts or segments of the data for specific users to utilize and analyze.

However, there are other times when the analyst may start out the process with the type of data they want and then they will use those specifications in order to create a warehouse. Regardless of how you plan to organize your data, you will use it to support the decision-making processes of the management.

Data mining programs are responsible for analyzing the relationships and patterns in data based on what the users request. For example, this software could be used in order to help create different classes of information. Imagine that there is a restaurant who decides to use this data mining to help them know when they should offer specials to their customers. This store would look at all the information that they have collected and then they can create some classes based on when the customers' visit and what things are ordered.

In some other instances, the data miner could find clusters of information that are based on logical relationships. They can choose to look at associations and sequential patterns in order to draw some conclusions about trends that show up in consumer behavior.

To keep things simple, the process of data mining is going to be broken down into five steps. These will include:

1. The organization will collect data before loading it into their data warehouses.
2. The company will store and manage the data. They can choose to store this data either in the cloud or in-house servers.
3. When this data is stored, information technology professionals, management teams, and business analysts will be able to access the data and determine the best way to organize it.
4. The application software will then sort out the data using the results it gets from the user.
5. The end user can then present this data in an easy-to-share format including a table or a graph.

Data mining can provide a lot of useful information to a business. It can help them learn more about their customers and make smart business decisions. Learning how to work with this tool and the software that comes with it can make a big difference in how the company will make important decisions.

The benefits of data mining

There are actually a lot of benefits that you will be able to enjoy when you work with data mining. In fact, almost every industry can benefit from this technique, as long as they learn how to use it properly. Some of the benefits of data mining includes:

- When talking about banking or finance, data mining is can be used to create some accurate risk models for mortgages and loans. They are also helpful when you are trying to detect if there is a fraudulent transaction.
- When it comes to marketing, data mining techniques can help increase the satisfaction of the customer, improve conversions, and create advertising campaigns that are highly targeted. They can even be utilized when the company needs to analyze the needs of the market or when they are trying to come up with some ideas for new product lines. This is done by taking a look at customer data and historical sales, and then using this information to create some powerful prediction models.
- Retail stores can use details about the shopping habits of their customers to help them improve the experience of customers, optimize how the store is set up, and to increase their profits.
- Tax governing bodies can use data mining techniques. They may find that this is useful with suspicious tax returns and fraudulent transactions.
- When it comes to manufacturing, data discovery is going to be used in order to improve the comfort, usability, and safety of the product.

As you can see, data mining is able to benefit everyone. Whether you are in charge of a large corporation or a smaller company, you will find that there is some use of data mining for you.

Examples of Questions in Data Mining

Data mining is a very wide topic that aims to find answers to issues such as:

1. Definition of data
2. Types of patterns that can be found in data
3. In which way can we use this data for future benefit?

Population and Sample

Data mining has extensive data sets, with millions of potential scenarios. However, each industry has its own condition, and most vary based on the countdown of the cases that will arise from the business processes. A great example is web applications, such as CRM, and data protection laws, as well as the local market and industry customs, which are all different. However, if we look at most countries, it is okay for one to buy or even rent the information at an aggregate level.

Data mining requires the use of scientific techniques to deal with massive data sets. Therefore, there is a lot of information, more than what we require. In some instances, our data set can be said to be larger. If we are handling little amounts of data, then we would prefer to deal with the entire data set. However, if we are dealing with a large data set, we can go with the subset to ease the manipulation. However, if we analyze the sample, the results found are a representative of a large population. In short, we can use the sample results as an inference of the rest of the population.

This means that we need to have a correct sample that can reveal the nature of the entire population. Therefore, we can say that the sample has to be unbiased. The sampling topic is very wide, and we cannot discuss everything here. Any time you are sampling a large population, you should extract large samples that give you the ability to select a sample randomly that contains members of a certain population.

Preparation of Data

In data mining, it is important for data to be prepared. This crucial step is sometimes ignored. Looking at our early years, we were taught 1+1=2. Numbers are considered solid, tangible, concrete as well as a means by which we can use to measure everything. However, numbers have a certain unique feature. For instance, it is possible to sale two products on the same day at a different price. Interpretations that are done just at face value are not enough. There are individual businesses that use data to make decisions, but they fail to ensure that the data is important. The businesses fail to change data into knowledge and intelligence.

Unsupervised and Supervised Approaches

We refer to data mining as a procedure that consists of different techniques of analysis to find unique, fascinating, and unexpected patterns that can help one develop correct and exact predictions. Generally, you will find that there are two methods of data analysis. One is called the *supervised* method while the other one is called the *unsupervised* method.

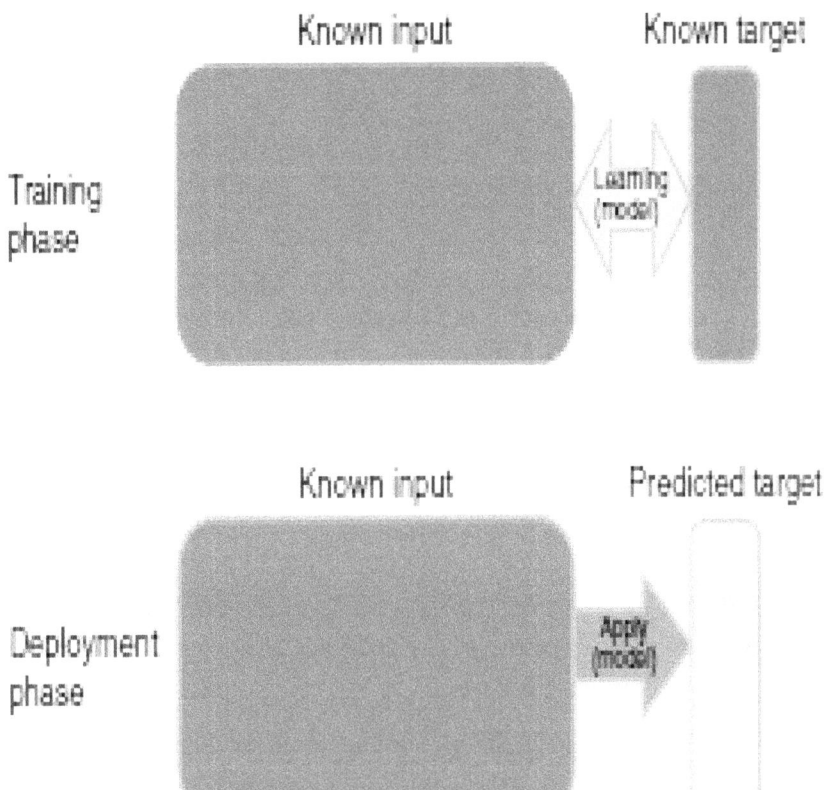

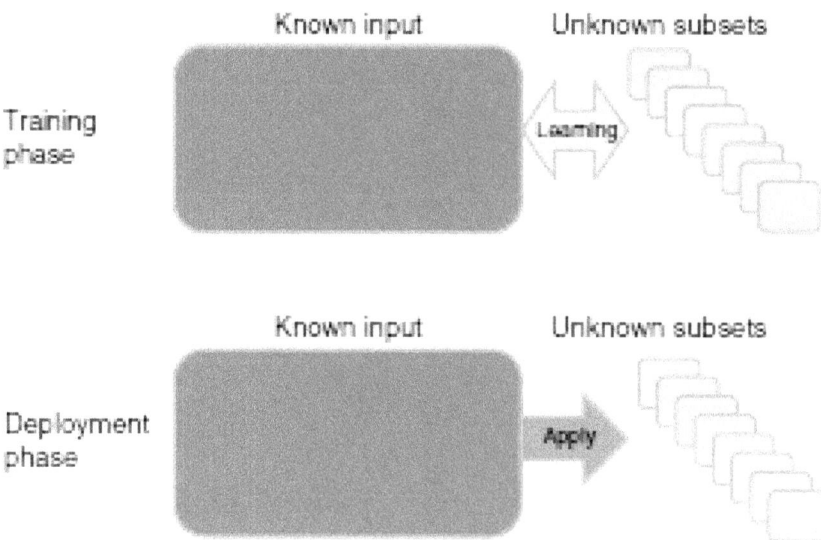

The *supervised* method allows you to make an estimate of unique dependency using data that is known. The input data could include quantities of different elements created by a specific customer, purchased date, location, and the price paid.

The output data might include something such as whether buyers can accept a specific sales campaign. We can refer to output variable as targets in the data mining. When we are dealing with a *supervised* environment, the selected sample input has to go through a given system of learning. When this is over, both the output and input are compared. This helps us determine whether customers can acknowledge a specific sale campaign.

Why Data Mining?

We live in a world where we have a lot of data generated as well as collected every day. Moreover, the need to analyze this kind of data is important. Therefore, with data mining, we get the chance to change a large data set into knowledge.

The search engine has millions of queries entered every day. We can look at each query as a transaction where the user can explain the information or their needs. Interestingly, we have certain patterns in the user search queries that can reveal crucial knowledge that no one can find by reading individual data items alone.

There are so many reasons why you would want to consider working with data mining. Right now, the volume of data that is being produced is doubling every two years, and the rate is likely to increase in the future. Unstructured data, on its own, is able to make up 90 percent of our digital universe. But more information doesn't always translate into more knowledge.

With the help of data mining, you will be able to do the following:

- Sift through all the noise that is repetitive and chaotic in the data you have in front of you.
- Understand what is relevant and then make good use of that information in order to help you assess the likely outcomes that will happen.
- Can accelerate how fast you are able to make decisions that are informed, thanks to the data that you know are available.

Who Uses Data mining?

The next question that you may have is, "Who would actually be able to use data mining?" This seems like a very analytical field, so you may assume that only businesses that rely on hard data all the time would want to use this. However, you will find that data mining can be at the heart of many types of analytical efforts, across many different disciplines and industries. Some of the different industries who benefit from using data mining include:

- Communications: In a market that is very overloaded and where the competition is fierce, the answers to help you get ahead and please your customers can often be found inside any consumer data you have. Telecommunication and multimedia companies can use various analytic models to help them make sense of all the customer data they have (and it is likely that they have a lot). This is a great way to help these companies predict how their customer will behave and can make it easier to create relevant and highly targeted campaigns.
- Insurance: With the right analytic know-how, insurance companies are then able to solve some complex problems that would include issues like customer attrition, risk management, compliance, and fraud. Insurance companies have been able to use many data mining techniques to help them in ways such as pricing product more effectively across the business and finding new ways that they can offer a product that is competitive to the customer base that they already have.
- Education: It is possible to use data mining with education. With a data-driven and unified view of the progress of each student, an educator can then predict how the student will perform before they even enter the classroom. This can be useful as the educator works to develop intervention strategies that will keep that student on course. Data mining can help educators access student data, predict achievement levels, and even pinpoint students or groups of students who may need a little extra time and attention.
- Manufacturing: aligning your supply plans with demand forecasts is so essential, as is the ability to detect problems early, investment in brand equity, and quality assurance. Manufacturers are able to use data mining in order to predict the status of production assets and anticipate when maintenance will be needed. This means that they are better able to maximize their uptime and make sure that the production line can stay on schedule.

- Banking: There are several automated algorithms that are able to help a bank understand their customer base, as well as the billions of transactions that are found in the financial system. Data mining can come in and help these financial companies in many ways. These include helping to detect fraud faster, giving the company a better view of their risks in the market, and even helping them to manage the regulatory compliance obligations that they have.
- Retail: Large databases of customers can hold a lot of insights for retail companies. If they are able to find this information, it can help improve customer relationships, optimize marketing campaigns, and even forecast sales. Through the accurate data models that they get from data mining, these retail companies will be able to offer more targeted campaigns and be better at finding the offer that will make the biggest impact on the customer.

How it works

Data mining, as a discipline that is composite, is going to represent a lot of different techniques and methods that can be used in different analytic capabilities. These are all there to help address a large amount of company needs that you may have. They are going to ask different types of questions, along with varying levels of human rules or inputs, to arrive at the answers that you are looking for. There are three main parts that come with it and these are:

Descriptive Modeling

This is going to take the time to uncover any shared similarities or groupings that show up in historical data. This is done in order to help the company determine what reasons there are behind a success or a failure. This process could include something like categorizing customers' product preferences or sentiment. Some of the sample techniques that are used for this include:

- Clustering: This is where you will group similar records together;
- Anomaly detection: Identifying multidimensional outliers;
- Association rule learning: Detecting relationships between the records;
- Principal component analysis: Detecting the relationship that is present between the variables; and
- Affinity grouping: This is when you group together people who have similar goals or common interests.

Predictive Modeling

This type of modeling is going to go deeper to help classify events in the future, or to estimate outcomes that are unknown. For example, it could work with a credit score in order to determine how likely it is that an individual would be able to repay their loan. Predictive modeling will also help uncover insights for things like credit defaults, campaign results, and customer churn. Some of the techniques that you can use with this type of modeling include:

- Regression: This is a measure of how strong a relationship is between one dependent variable to a series of independent variables;
- Neural networks: These are computer programs that are there to detect patterns, make predictions, and then learn;
- Decision trees: These are diagrams that are shaped like trees where each branch is going to represent an occurrence that is probable; and
- Support vector machines: These are supervised learning models that have associated learning algorithms.

Prescriptive Modeling

With the growth of much unstructured data that comes from audio, PDF's, books, email, comment fields, the web, and other sources of text, the adoption of text mining, a discipline found within data mining, has seen a huge amount of growth. You must have the ability to successfully parse, filter, and then transform this unstructured data in order to include this data in your predictive models to get an accurate prediction.

In the end, you do not want to look at data mining and then assume that it is a standalone entity because pre-processing and post-processing are going to be pretty equal. Prescriptive modeling is going to look at the internal and external variables and the constraints to help you get recommendations on one or more courses of actions. This could include using it to determine which marketing offer is the best one to send out to each of your customers. Some of the techniques that are included in prescriptive modeling include:

- Predictive analytics plus rules: This is where you develop if/then rules from patterns and then predict the outcomes.
- Marketing optimization: Simulating the most advantageous media mix in real time in order to get the highest possible return on investment.

Chapter 2: Know Your Data

It is important to make sure that the data is ready. This means that we need to review the data values and attributes. Real-world data is noisy and large, and there are times when it can emerge from random sources.

This chapter will help you familiarize with your data. Having a better understanding of your data is critical when it comes to data processing. This is the first important step when it comes to the data mining process. Some fields that make up your data are:

- The type of values of each attribute.
- Find out continuous and discrete attributes.
- Is there a way for us to visualize the data so that we can look at the data to get some meanings from it?
- Can we identify some of the outliers?
- Can we examine some of the similarities of the data objects with others?

If you can develop this kind of insight, it will help in the rest of the analysis.

Now you might ask yourself, *What do I need to know about data that is critical in the preprocessing?* We will start by looking at different types of attributes. Some of these comprise of the binary attributes, nominal attributes, numeric attributes and ordinal attributes. We will review a few standard descriptions so that we can understand better the values of the attributes.

For instance, if you have a temperature attribute, it is possible to determine the mean, mode, and median temperature.

Having a basic understanding of these statistics based on each attribute makes everything simple to help fill any missing values as well as identify any strange attributes in the data processing. Knowing the attributes as well as the attribute values can drastically contribute towards repairing abnormalities that happened in the data integration. By using the mean, median and mode, it helps reveal if the data is symmetrical or lop-sided. The field of visualizing data has numerous techniques. This will help see the biases, trends, and relations.

In other words, before the end of this chapter, you will have interacted with several attribute types and some of the standard statistical measures to help define the central tendency as well as the dispersion.

Data Objects and Types of Attributes

Data sets have data objects. A data object describes an entity. If we take an example of a sales database, we can have objects like customers and sales. If we have a sports database, the objects could be players, teams and so on. If the database belongs to a college or a university, examples of objects include courses, lecturers, and students.

The data objects are often described by attributes. The data objects could also be described as attributes. Furthermore, we can call them instances, samples, or even data points. When we store the data objects in a database, we refer to them as data tuples. That means database rows are similar to data objects and the column is similar to the attributes.

Attribute

An attribute is simply a data field that shows the features of a data object. Professionals in data mining as well as in the data mining field interact several times with the term attribute. An attribute that describes an object of type customer can include the following: customer ID, address, and name. Observations refer to values observed for a specific attribute. The set of attributes normally used to describe a precise object is called attribute vector. Data distribution of a single attribute is called univariate. Distribution of two values is called bivariate. An attribute type is defined by a collection of possible values – binary, numeric, ordinal, and nominal.

Nominal Attributes

A nominal attribute is one that is associated with the names. Nominal attributes carry with it the names of things or even symbols. Every value will show some type of state, category and hence nominal attributes are called categorical.

Example of nominal attributes

Let us consider team color and team_perfomance, which are attributes that describe a soccer team. If we are to build an application, the potential values for the team color could be blue, gray, white, and brown. Similarly, the attributes for the team_perfomance could include fair, incredible, average, or excellent.

Even though we had previously mentioned that the nominal attributes refer to symbols and names of things, we can still represent these symbols. A good example is with the team color as we can assign it some codes. We can look at another example like the customer ID with all the possible values as numeric. However, in this case, the numbers should not be used quantitatively.

Since values of a nominal attribute are not that significant, there is no need to determine the median or mean value for this type of attribute if you have a collection of objects at your disposal. One thing that is significant is the most frequent value of the attribute. This is referred to as the mode and belongs to the measures of central tendency.

Binary Attributes

For the binary attribute, we have two types of states: 0 or 1. In this case, 0 represents a missing attribute while 1 shows that the attribute exists.

Chapter 3: Data Preparation

The raw nature of the actual data is different in many ways. Most values could be missing, others inconsistent and some even contain errors. For a data analyst, this creates many problems in using the data most effectively. Let us take an example of analyzing consumer's interest based on their different tasks on social networks. The analyst may want to define operations that are central to the mining process. Some of these operations may have specific user interests, like the friends of the user. For this case, each of this set of information is different and has to be gathered from separate databases on the social network site.

In addition, there are specific elements of information that cannot be used directly because of its nature. Instead, critical traits of information should be extracted from the data sources. This is when data preparation becomes important.

The data preparation stage is multiple processes made up of individual steps. Some of the steps may or may not be applied in one application.

1. Portability and Extraction of Properties

Typically, it is hard to process raw data because of its initial form. Some forms of raw data include semi-structured data, raw logs, and many others. Because of the inability to process raw data, it is important to extract major features from the data. Generally, you will realize that data properties that have the correct interpretability are far much better because they help make it easy for a person to understand results.

Besides, they are bounded by the data mining application goals. In situations where data comes from multiple places, data has to be integrated into one database to help in the processing. Furthermore, there are specific algorithms that work with data that has heterogeneous types. Here the portability of data is important when we change one attribute into another. This builds a uniform data set, which algorithms can now process.

2. Cleaning Data

In this step, we remove errors and unpredictable data entries. In addition, it is during this step that we perform imputation. There are so many reasons why you would want to consider working with data mining. Right now, the volume of data that is being produced is doubling every two years, and the rate is likely to increase in the future. Unstructured data, on its own, is able to make up 90 percent of our digital universe. But more information doesn't always translate into more knowledge.

With the help of data mining, you will be able to do the following:

- Sift through all the noise that is repetitive and chaotic in the data you have in front of you.
- Understand what is relevant and then make good use of that information in order to help you assess the likely outcomes that will happen.
- Can accelerate how fast you are able to make decisions that are informed, thanks to the data that you know are available.

Who Uses Data mining?

The next question that you may have is, "Who would actually be able to use data mining?" This seems like a very analytical field, so you may assume that only businesses that rely on hard data all the time would want to use this. However, you will find that data mining can be at the heart of many types of analytical efforts, across many different disciplines and industries. Some of the different industries who benefit from using data mining include:

- Communications: In a market that is very overloaded and where the competition is fierce, the answers to help you get ahead and please your customers can often be found inside any consumer data you have. Telecommunication and multimedia companies can use various analytic models to help them make sense of all the customer data they have (and it is likely that they have a lot). This is a great way to help these companies predict how their customer will behave and can make it easier to create relevant and highly targeted campaigns.
- Insurance: With the right analytic know-how, insurance companies are then able to solve some complex problems that would include issues like customer attrition, risk management, compliance, and fraud. Insurance companies have been able to use many data mining techniques to help them in ways such as pricing product more effectively across the business and finding new ways that they can offer a product that is competitive to the customer base that they already have.
- Education: It is possible to use data mining with education. With a data-driven and unified view of the progress of each student, an educator can then predict how the student will perform before they even enter the classroom. This can be useful as the educator works to develop intervention strategies that will keep that student on course. Data mining can help educators access student data, predict achievement levels, and even pinpoint students or groups of students who may need a little extra time and attention.

- Manufacturing: aligning your supply plans with demand forecasts is so essential, as is the ability to detect problems early, investment in brand equity, and quality assurance. Manufacturers are able to use data mining in order to predict the status of production assets and anticipate when maintenance will be needed. This means that they are better able to maximize their uptime and make sure that the production line can stay on schedule.
- Banking: There are several automated algorithms that are able to help a bank understand their customer base, as well as the billions of transactions that are found in the financial system. Data mining can come in and help these financial companies in many ways. These include helping to detect fraud faster, giving the company a better view of their risks in the market, and even helping them to manage the regulatory compliance obligations that they have.
- Retail: Large databases of customers can hold a lot of insights for retail companies. If they are able to find this information, it can help improve customer relationships, optimize marketing campaigns, and even forecast sales. Through the accurate data models that they get from data mining, these retail companies will be able to offer more targeted campaigns and be better at finding the offer that will make the biggest impact on the customer.

How it works

Data mining, as a discipline that is composite, is going to represent a lot of different techniques and methods that can be used in different analytic capabilities. These are all there to help address a large amount of company needs that you may have. They are going to ask different types of questions, along with varying levels of human rules or inputs, to arrive at the answers that you are looking for. There are three main parts that come with it and these are:

Descriptive Modeling

This is going to take the time to uncover any shared similarities or groupings that show up in historical data. This is done in order to help the company determine what reasons there are behind a success or a failure. This process could include something like categorizing customers' product preferences or sentiment. Some of the sample techniques that are used for this include:

- Clustering: This is where you will group similar records together;
- Anomaly detection: Identifying multidimensional outliers;
- Association rule learning: Detecting relationships between the records;
- Principal component analysis: Detecting the relationship that is present between the variables; and
- Affinity grouping: This is when you group together people who have similar goals or common interests.

Predictive Modeling

This type of modeling is going to go deeper to help classify events in the future, or to estimate outcomes that are unknown. For example, it could work with a credit score in order to determine how likely it is that an individual would be able to repay their loan. Predictive modeling will also help uncover insights for things like credit defaults, campaign results, and customer churn. Some of the techniques that you can use with this type of modeling include:

- Regression: This is a measure of how strong a relationship is between one dependent variable to a series of independent variables;
- Neural networks: These are computer programs that are there to detect patterns, make predictions, and then learn;
- Decision trees: These are diagrams that are shaped like trees where each branch is going to represent an occurrence that is probable; and
- Support vector machines: These are supervised learning models that have associated learning algorithms.

Prescriptive Modeling

With the growth of much unstructured data that comes from audio, PDF's, books, email, comment fields, the web, and other sources of text, the adoption of text mining, a discipline found within data mining, has seen a huge amount of growth. You must have the ability to successfully parse, filter, and then transform this unstructured data in order to include this data in your predictive models to get an accurate prediction.

In the end, you do not want to look at data mining and then assume that it is a standalone entity because pre-processing and post-processing are going to be pretty equal. Prescriptive modeling is going to look at the internal and external variables and the constraints to help you get recommendations on one or more courses of actions. This could include using it to determine which marketing offer is the best one to send out to each of your customers. Some of the techniques that are included in prescriptive modeling include:

- Predictive analytics plus rules: This is where you develop if/then rules from patterns and then predict the outcomes.
- Marketing optimization: Simulating the most advantageous media mix in real time in order to get the highest possible return on investment.

3. Selecting, Reducing, and Transforming Data

This phase reduces the scope of the data through transformation and subset selection of its features. This phase has two advantages. First, when we reduce the size of the data, we enhance the algorithm efficiency.

The second advantage is superfluous records which are eliminated, thereby enhancing the aesthetic nature of the mining process. The first advantage is realized through generic sampling as well as dimensionality reduction mechanism. To realize the second advantage, we have to use an advanced technique to select the features.

Mining of features and portability

The first thing to do in data mining is to create a collection of features that will assist an analyst. Instances where data is in the raw form require the removal of features during the processing. In case we have a uniform state of features in diverse forms then an 'off-the-shelf' approach is not the best. Instead, it is recommended to convert data into an identical or uniform representation.

Feature Extraction

It is important to be aware that the first step in feature extraction is critical, whether or not it depends on the application. In some cases, feature extraction is identical to data portability where low-level features are changed into a higher advanced feature.

1. Sensor data

This type of data is collected in the form of low-level signals. You can still change the signals into an advanced feature using Fourier transforms. Sometimes the time series is used after data cleaning is over.

The sensors can be used in order to detect any kind of physical element that you would like. Some of the different examples of sensors that you can use to help you give an idea of the different applications of these sensors includes:

- Accelerometer: This sensor is able to detect the gravitational acceleration in any device that has it installed. This could include things like a game controller or a smartphone. It is good at determining things like vibration, tilt, and acceleration.
- Photosensor: This is going to have the ability to detect the presence of visible light, UV energy, and infrared transmission.
- Lidar: This is a laser-based method of detection, range finding and mapping, and it is often going to use a low-power, eye safe pulsing laser that works along with a camera.
- CCD: This is known as a charge coupled device and can store and display your data from an image in a way that each of the pixels in the image will be converted to an electrical charge. The intensity of these charges will be related to a color inside the color spectrum.
- Smart grid: These sensors are able to provide you with real time data about grid conditions so that you can check for outages, faults, load, and triggering alarms.

2. Image data

It is represented in pixels in its primitive form. In the advanced levels, we use the color histograms to represent the features in different image segment. Recently, the use of visual words has increased in popularity. This is a semantic representation similar to document data. One great challenge when it comes to image processing is the high dimensional nature of the data. Thus, one can use extracted features at different points based on the application.

3. Weblogs

These appear as text strings. If you want to change weblogs into a multidimensional form, that process is easy.

4. Network traffic

When it comes to detecting a form of intrusion in a network, the general network state of packets is important if you want to examine intrusions and other activities. Depending on the type of applications, we can identify different characteristics of the packets.

5. Document data

This exists in unstructured and raw form. The data can contain several linguistic associations between entities. One technique is to eliminate stem data and use a collection of words. Other techniques involve the application of entity extraction to create a linguistic relationship.

When it comes to feature extraction, it is a technique that depends on the data analyst to find out the traits and properties that fit the type of operation at hand. Although this field is suited for a given domain, the analysis can only be good based on the features that are extracted.

Data type portability

This is yet another important step in the data mining process because a big percentage of the data is mixed, and may be different. For example, the data set of a demographic place could contain both numerals and mixed features. With this kind of variation in the data set, it requires the analyst to design an efficient algorithm that can integrate all the combinations of the data types. Extraction of data types again prohibits the analyst from applying the off-the-shelf processing tools.

In this section, we shall look at the methods one can use to convert different data types. Given that the numeric data type is one of the most widely used mining algorithms, one should concentrate on how to convert different types of data. Besides this, the remaining conversion types are still important. For example, in the similarity algorithms, you can convert a data type into a graph and use algorithms to represent it.

Discretization

One of the most popular types of conversion is numerical to categorical data type conversion. This is where different values of ranges are divided into φT ranges. This property has diverse categorized values that begin from 1 to φ, subject to the initial attribute range.

During the process of discretization, information is lost in the mining process. However, we have applications where information loss is not that devastating. The major disadvantage is that we can have data that is randomly spread at separate intervals. One example to consider is the salary attribute.

Similarly, age attribute is not uniformly spread, and this means that a range of equal size could work out well. Discretization has no single way that it can be done. In fact, there are many ways subject to the particular application of the goal.

1. Equi-width ranges

Here we have a range of [a, b] selected where b-a are the same for each interval. The weakness of this method is that it cannot be possible to use it on data sets with properties that are randomly spread out at different intervals. To find out the initial range value, we have to make sure that we define the lowest and highest value of each property. After this, we can divide both the min and max value into a range of equal size.

2. Equi-log ranges

In this case, each interval in [a, b] is selected such that if we subtract log(b)-log(a) we get the same value. This tends to have the characteristics of an increasing range [a1, a2, a3] for a > 1. This kind of range is applied whenever an attribute shows features of exponential distribution across a given range.

3. Equi-depth ranges

This type of range requires a range to be selected. The range that is chosen has to have the same number of records. The basic idea is to ensure that you create a level of similarity on each range. We can divide a given property into equal range divisions by performing a sort and finally pick the division points on each property value that is sorted.

Binarization

There are times when it is important to apply numeric algorithms on a specific data. You can do this because of the differences that exist between binary data and other data types such as numeric data and categorical data. If you would like, you can convert a categorical data type into a binary data type. If it happens that the categorical property of the data has foreign attributes, then it is necessary to produce a foreign binary property. Each attribute is the same as the value of the categorical attribute.

Converting text into numeric data

While the text representation is a sparse numeric set which contains advanced dimensions, it is not that popular compared to the general data mining algorithms. For example, an individual may decide to use a cosine function instead of applying the Euclidean distance for every text data. This is one of the reasons why text mining is unique, and it has its own algorithms. Regardless of that, you can change a set of text into something that is popular with the numerical algorithms. First, apply some semantic analysis to help change a set of text into a lower dimension. Once you are through with transformation, you can start to scale.

Convert time series into discrete data sequence

If you want to change a time series data into a discrete data sequence, there are two approaches to take. Both methods are briefly described below:

1. Window-based averaging

In this method, there exists the length of the window w, and the average time-series of every calculated window.

2. Value-based discretization

This method will first divide time series values into smaller chunks of equal intervals, similar to the equi-depth discretization approach used in the numeric properties. The point to take into consideration is that each symbol carriers an equal time series frequency. Interval boundaries are created by making an assumption. The assumption is that the values of the time series are distributed through the Gaussian method. In each case, we compute the standard deviation as well as the mean of the time series so that we can assign parameters to the Gaussian distribution. Quantiles defined through the Gaussian distribution are important when one wants to set up the boundaries of the intervals. Usually, this is much better compared to sorting all the data values.

Converting time series data into numeric

This is very important because it helps one get the chance to make use of multidimensional algorithms. The discrete wavelength transform is used in the following approach. The wavelength transform changes the time series data into multidimensional data, a collection of coefficients, which display the average difference between separate portions of the series.

Convert discrete data into numeric data

This kind of conversion can take place in two different ways. The first one is to change the discrete sequence into a binary time series. This type of conversion has the number of time series equivalent to the number of unique symbols.

The second way is where we map individual time series values into a multidimensional vector. This is done with the help of a wavelet transform. Lastly, we combine all the time series features into a single large record.

To change an order into a binary time series, it is important for one to build a binary string that can define whether a given symbol is present in a specific position.

Spatial to numeric data

It is possible to change spatial data into numeric by using a similar approach used to convert time-series data type. The only exception in this type of conversion is the existence of two major properties that requires a modification to the wavelet transformation.

Convert graphs into numeric data

It is possible to change data in the graph into numeric data by applying several methods such as multidimensional scaling. Most of these methods are suited in applications where we have the edges weighted. In addition, there exist some distance relationships. The most spectral approach can be applied in converting a graph into a multidimensional representation.

Cleaning of Data

This process is key because of the mistakes and inconsistency in the data collection process. A few missing errors and entries might arise in the collection process. Some of the examples include:

1. There are certain data collection technologies that are never accurate because of the hardware limitations related to the transmission and collection. For instance, sensors can skip a reading because of battery exhaustion or hardware challenges.
2. Data that is gathered using the scanning technologies might contain errors because the optical character device might have errors. In addition, speech to text data contains errors.
3. Users might avoid describing their information because of privacy, or they might say incorrect details.
4. A reasonable size of data is produced manually. Manual errors are prone in the process of data entry.
5. The entry defined for data collection might not have fields for certain records that appear expensive. Thus, we can have records that are not well specified.

The issues listed above could affect the accuracy of the data mining applications. Therefore, methods are required to correct the errors and missing values in a data. Below are some of the listed properties in data mining:

1. Dealing with missing values

Many data records have less information because of the disadvantages in the process of collecting data or the overall nature of the data. These types of entries require estimation. The procedure of approximating entries is called imputation.

2. Dealing with incorrect entries

In situations where we have similar information from different sources, it is possible to detect inconsistency. The analytical process involves removal of such inconsistencies.

3. Data scaling and normalization

Data can be expressed in different forms. This can result in certain features getting much more attention than others. It is, therefore, a good practice to learn to normalize separate features.

Let us look at each of the aspects of data cleaning mentioned above in detail.

1. Dealing with missing entries

Instances of missing entries are prominent in databases that have a wrong method of data collection. Examples are user surveys that cannot allow one to collect responses to all questions. Three techniques can be used to correct omitted or misplaced entries:

> 1. A data record that has missing entries is removed completely. However, this method might not be the best when most records have misplaced entries.
> 2. Omitted values should be assigned. However, errors that can arise through imputation can interfere with the data mining algorithm.
> 3. The analytical method is created in a way where it can deal with missing values. A lot of the data mining techniques work excellently when we have misplaced values. This is the best approach because it limits biases in the imputation phase.

The challenge that exists while approximating entries is similar to that in classification. A single attribute is assumed unique, and the remaining values define the estimate of the value. Therefore, a misplaced value could appear on whichever property, and this makes the problem more difficult.

When we consider spatial data and time series data, it is easy to approximate a misplaced value. In this instance, behavioral values are used during the imputation phase.

How to deal with missing entries

The major methods used to correct and remove inconsistent entries include:

1. Detection of inconsistency

This is achieved when data from different format sources are present. For instance, the name of a person might be written in full while the remaining sources might have symbols for initials and last name alone. In this example, the major concern is the detection of inconsistency and duplicate.

2. Domain knowledge

A considerable size of the domain knowledge exists based on the range of the attributes. An example is that if the country is the United States, then the city cannot be 'Dubai'. Many of the data auditing and scrubbing tools are designed to use the domain constraints and knowledge to control incorrect entries.

3. Data-centric methods

This method applies statistical data behavior to define outliers.

Scaling and Normalization

Most of the time, different features display separate scales of reference, and it is hard to compare one to another. For instance, the age attribute is defined on a separate scale different from a salary attribute.

Transformation and Reduction of Data

The concept behind data reduction is to show it compactly. In the case when the size of the data is small, it is not hard to use expensive or complex algorithms. The data may be reduced in the form of rows or columns. The reduction of data does not lead to information loss, but the use of an advanced algorithm can cause the loss of information. Below are some of the techniques to use in data reduction:

1. Data sampling

In this method, hidden data records are extracted to help make a small size database. In general, it is difficult to sample streaming data because the sample has to be updated dynamically.

2. Feature selection

This is where we select a small subset of the data features and apply it in the analytical process. Selecting a subset is carried out in an application-dependent way. This is because a method that might work in clustering may fail to apply during classification.

3. Data Reduction

The relationship existing in data is to help reveal a few dimensions. If you want to reduce data, you can decide to use semantic analysis, latent analysis and other methods not mentioned here.

4. Data reduction based on the type of transformation

This data type is associated with type portability.

Chapter 4: Similarity and Distances

Most of how data mining is applied requires a way of creating a distinction between similar attributes, patterns, and events present in data. It is a way where you can find out the similarity between data objects. Nearly all problems experienced in data mining have some similarity.

With the similarity functions, you will notice that bigger values have a greater similarity and the converse is true when it comes to functions related to distance. Other fields, such as the spatial data, distance functions are the most popularly discussed, while in the text domain, similarity functions take the lead. Not only that but also the principles used in the development of these functions are all different.

This chapter will look at some of the functions related to distance and similarity. Both of these functions appear in closed form except in specific domains where we have the time series data determined algorithmically.

Distance functions are critical when it comes to the design of the data mining algorithms. One of the reasons for this is that a poor choice will adversely affect the quality of the results. There are situations when a data analyst will use the Euclidean function without taking into consideration the general choice. In general, it is a rare choice for a less experienced analyst to dedicate a lot of effort in the design of algorithm when dealing with the distance function.

Multidimensional Data

Even though multidimensional data looks simple, there is a lot of difference in the distance function design when we consider attribute types like qualitative or categorical data.

Quantitative Data

The Lp-norm is the most popular type of distance function used to deal with the quantitative data. We define the Lp-norm of two data points such as point X and Y in the following way:

$$Dist(\overline{X},\overline{Y}) = \left(\sum_{i=1}^{d} |x_i - y_i|^p\right)^{1/p}.$$

The two instances of the Lp-norm include the Euclidean and Manhattan metrics. Both of these cases are unique. A straight line that joins two data points is called the Euclidean distance while the distance around a region organized in a rectangular shape is the Manhattan distance.

Rotation-invariant is a property of the Euclidean distance, which cannot affect the nature of a given system. This feature has it that changes in the PCA, SVD, and wavelet transformation should be excluded from distance. Another important situation has to do with setting $p = \infty$. This type of computation creates two objects that are far from one another and display the absolute value of the distance.

When dealing with the Lp-norm, it is a popular distance function used in data mining. It is common because of its natural intuitive appeal and the interpretability of the L1 and L2 norms when used in spatial applications. However, the natural interpretation of the above distances does not mean that they are the most important ones. Furthermore, these functions might fail to work correctly whenever the data is high dimensional.

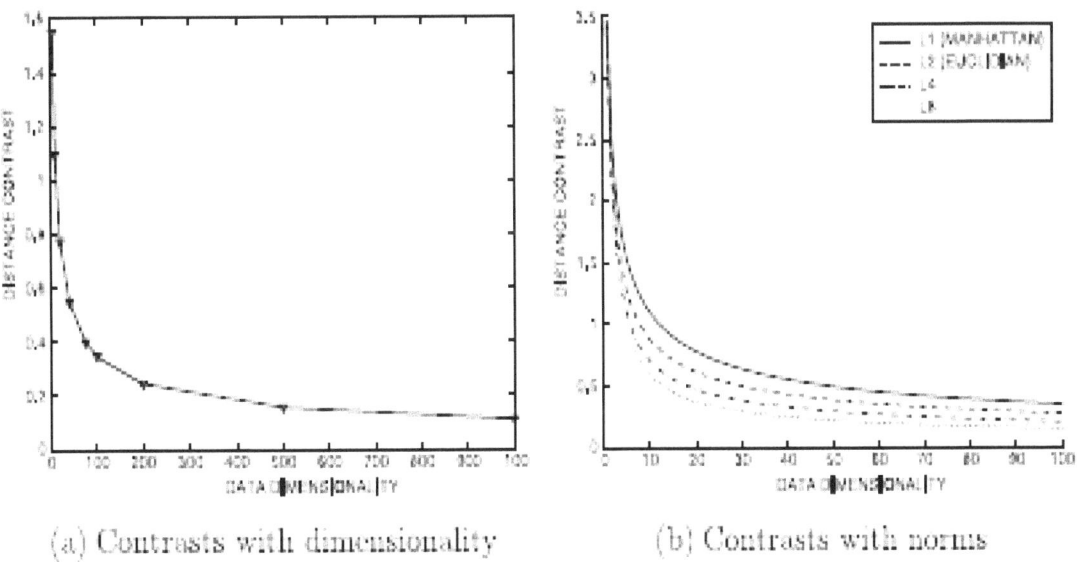

(a) Contrasts with dimensionality   (b) Contrasts with norms

The above figure shows how a reduction in distance varies with the increase in dimensions and norms.

The impact of domain Specific Relevance

In some instances, it is possible for the analyst to tell the type of features that are important from others in a specific application. For instance, when we look at a credit-scoring software, the salary attribute is important when we design the system as well as the distance function. This is not the same as a gender property that can have several differences.

In the following case, the analyst might decide to measure the property differently in case there exists a domain-specific knowledge. Usually, this heuristic procedure depends on the skill and experiences. The generalized Lp-distance is the best for this situation, and it is definite in the same way to the Lp-norm, the only difference is that the coefficient a1 is related to the 'ith' property. The same factor is used to calculate the weight of the related feature in the Lp-norm.

$$Dist(\overline{X}, \overline{Y}) = \left(\sum_{i=1}^{d} a_i \cdot |x_i - y_i|^p \right)^{1/p}$$

Most of the time, this domain knowledge does not exist. In this case, the Lp-norm can be the default state. However, when there is no knowledge related to the key features, the Lp-norm becomes vulnerable to the effects of dimensions.

The Impact of High Dimensionality

If you look at the application cases for the distance-based data mining, you will realize that efficiency decreases with the increase in dimensionality. We can consider a distance algorithm designed for clustering; this algorithm can create special data points because of the increase in dimension. This means that the distance-based model of classification and clustering are inefficient qualitatively. This is also called the "curse of dimensionality".

The Effect of Locally Irrelevant Features

One of the major ways of assessing the impact created by high dimensionality is analyzing unnecessary features. This is important because all properties will be different in a large data set. An example is a database containing patients' medical history records.

A distance metric may result in a high value emerging from the noisy modules. The key factor is that the exact characteristics important to the distance computation may be sensitive to a specific pair of objects compared. It is hard for the global feature subset to solve this problem because the importance of the features is defined locally using a pair of objects. In general, virtually all the features may be unnecessary.

Whenever we have many irrelevant features, the unnecessary features are represented in distances. In many cases, these unnecessary characteristics might result in errors while calculating the distance. Since a high dimensional data set can have separate features, and many of these features are not relevant, the additive effect may not be that worse.

The effect of Different Lp-norms

Different Lp-norms do not work in the same manner like distance contrast or irrelevant features. You can consider the worst case where $p = \infty$. This results in the use of a dimension where two objects are not the same. In most cases, this could be the result of a normal variation in an odd property not necessary in the similarity applications.

Calculation of a match in similarity

Since it is advised to choose locally appropriate features for a given distance calculation, a question that has to be addressed is how this can be possible in data mining. An easy way to approach it is by assuming the aggregate evidence of comparing various characteristic values that have been found to be efficient. In addition, the technique is not hard to implement. The most important thing that works perfectly for high-dimensional data are the effects caused by variations in noise and the individual attributes. Normally, this type of approach creates many challenges for low-dimensional data. Therefore, a technique is required to modify the dimensions of the data automatically. With an increase in the dimensionality, a record can have both true and false properties. A pair of semantic objects may have different values due to the difference in noise.

At the same time, a pair of objects might have values that are similar and cover a wide property. Most fascinating is that the Euclidean metric uses a completely different effect. This causes the noise modules from the odd features to take up a large space and translate the same relevant attributes.

The $L\infty$-norm is a good example to use to indicate the dimension that has the largest distance value. In the advanced domains, there seems to be an emphasis on the aggregate impact of a match on numerous values rather than large distances in an individual property. You can also use the same principle in quantitative data.

One way to stress the exact levels of dissimilarity is with the help of proximity thresholding. To achieve this, it is important for the data to be kept in the discrete state. Each dimension is divided into kd equi-depth buckets. The number of buckets depends on the data dimensions.

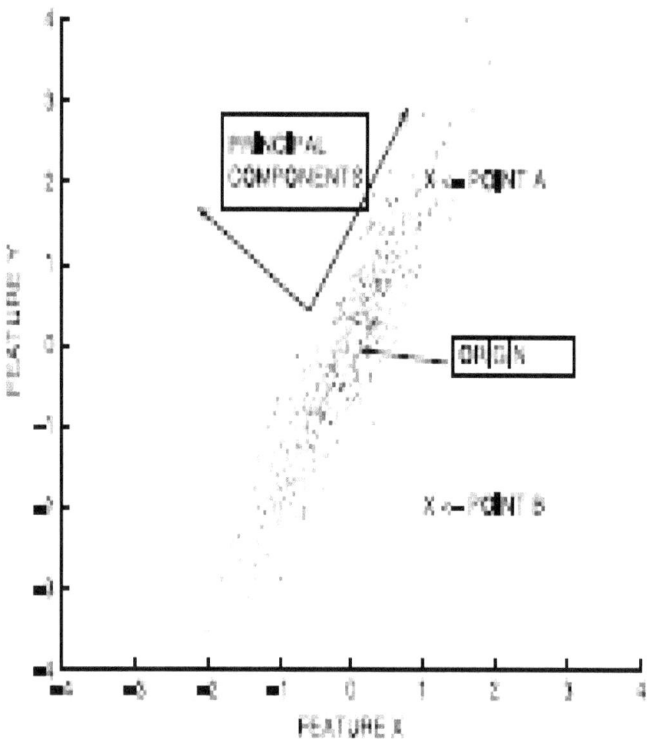

Global data distributions impact distance computations

The Effect of Data Distribution

The Lp-norm relies on only two data points, and it has an indirect relationship to the global statistics of the rest of the points. This means that the distance depends on how data is spread out in the data set. To show this, you should refer to the distribution shown below. Besides that, the two data points A and B have been demonstrated in the previous diagram. As you can see, both points A and B are equidistant from the origin depending on the Lp-norm.

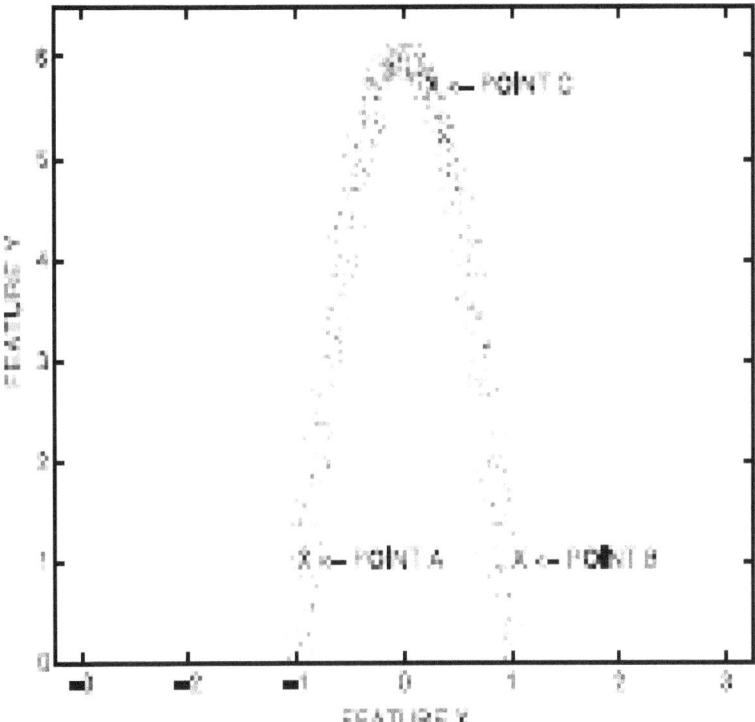

Impact of nonlinear distributions on distance computations

One major question of concern is whether the points A and B are equidistant from the center. The answer to this is that we have a line running from O to A that is equal to the highest change in direction in the data, and there is a likely chance for the data points to be far in this case. Likewise, many parts that run from O to B are not densely populated. In addition, we have the equivalent direction as a point of low variance. This means a comparison has to be carried out between O to A and that from O to B.

The 'Mahalanobis distance' is designed depending on this principle. If you want to understand the Mahalanobis distance, you have to look at it on the grounds of component analysis. This distance is the same as the Euclidean distance with the only exception that it standardizes the data depending on the associations between attributes. For example, if we need to rotate the axis to the principal direction of the data, that data should be without the inter-attribute associations.

The nonlinear Distributions: ISOMAP

We want to consider a case where the data has a nonlinear distribution of any shape. A great example is the global distribution illustrated in the figure below. Based on the three data points shown above, which pair do you think is near to the other one? At first, you may say that A and B are the nearest; however, the global distribution is different. One approach to apply in understanding distances is through finding the shortest length from one point to another.

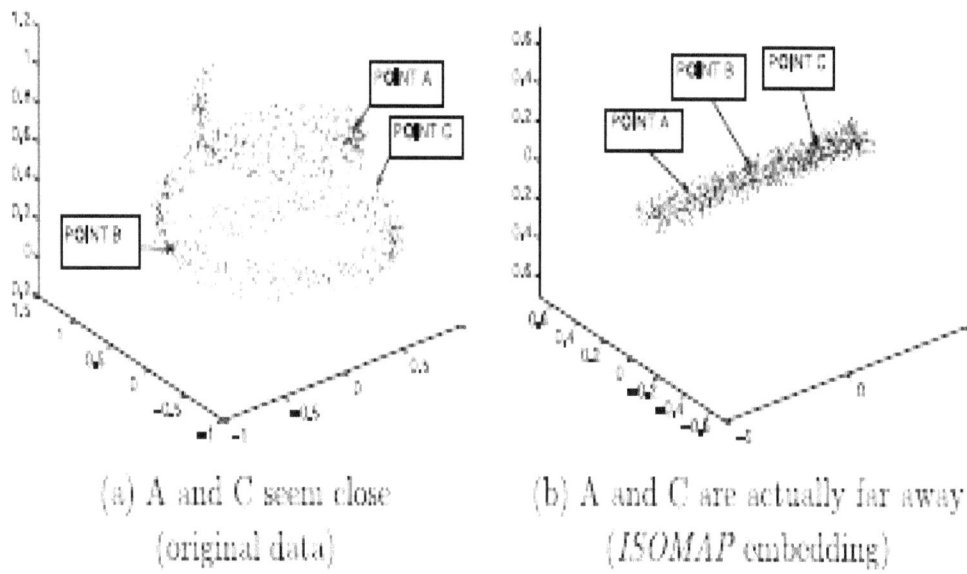

(a) A and C seem close (original data)

(b) A and C are actually far away (ISOMAP embedding)

The main concept for this is that only short point jumps allow one to measure smaller changes that occur in the generative process. Therefore, the total sum of jumping from one point to another is the cumulative change from one region to another.

Local Data Distribution Effect

The present discussion examines the effect of global distributions in calculating distance, but data distribution varies with locality. This type of change exists in two variations. For example, the data density may change depending on the shape or location of the data clusters.

Shared nearest neighbor relation

This situation involves the k-nearest neighbor of every data point calculated before the processing phase. This type of similarity is not different from the total sum of points close to the data points. In fact, it is more sensitive since it relies on the sum of shared neighbors as well as the absolute distances. In the highly-populated areas, k-nearest neighbor distance is small while the data points are near to increase the total sum of neighbors. The shared nearest neighbor can be used to define the graph similarity subject to the data points.

Generic methods

In this type of computation, the most important thing is to share the space into different local regions. Then we can modify the distance in each region with the help of a few statistics. In short, the main concept is this:

      1. Separate data into different local parts.
      2. Search for the most region in each partitioned data and calculate the distances of the region.
      3. Finally, divide separate sets of local regions

Several clustering approaches have been used to subdivide data into separate parts. Instances where each pair of objects come from a unique point, we resort to either use the general distribution or calculate the average. Another problem that could arise in the first step involves the dividing of the algorithm. This process usually creates a circular solution that needs an iterative solution.

Computational Considerations

When it comes to the development of distance functions, the major focus is on the computational intricacy. This is for the reason that computation of the distance is rooted on the subroutine, which depends on the current application. If the subroutine is not executed correctly, the application is limited. To use methods like ISOMAP is costlier and hard to execute for a huge data set. However, the great advantage with these methods is that a single change may build a representation that can be applied in the data mining algorithms correctly.

The distance functions are regularly used, but only the preprocessing occurs once. In short, it is beneficial to use preprocessing – intensive method if it is going to increase the computations. In most applications, complex methods like the ISOMAP may look more expensive although it is just for a single analysis.

Categorical Data

We calculate the distance functions as functions of value differences. However, no order exists in the distinct values of the categorical data. So, how can we compute the distance? One way is to convert data in categorical form into numeric form by use of the Binarization technique. Given that there is room for a binary vector to be sparse, you can opt to use similarity functions from other fields like text. For instance, if you are dealing with data in the categorical form, you will mostly use similarity functions instead of the distance functions because you can create a comparison of the discrete functions.

Quantitative and Categorical data

It is much easy to develop a generalized style for the mixed data by tallying the weights of the quantitative components and numeric components. The major task is in the way you will assign both the quantitative and categorical weight elements.

For instance, if we take two records of X and Y to be the subset of numerical attributes and X_c, Y_c are the subset of the categorical attributes, the general similarity will look like this:

$Sim(X, Y) = \lambda \cdot NumSim(X_n, Y_n) + (1 - \lambda) \cdot CatSim(X_c, Y_c)$.

The parameter λh usually defines the relevance of the numerical and categorical properties. This value of λ is not that easy especially when there is no domain knowledge.

A normal value for λv should be equivalent to the section of the numerical properties in the data. Besides that, the distance of the numerical data is found by computing the distance instead of the similarity functions.

Still, we can change the distance values. In addition, normalization is required so that a comparison is created between the similarity values of the components. A better approach is to identify the standard differences between the corresponding values of two domains.

Text Similarity Measures

We can assume text as quantitative multidimensional data if we review it comprehensively. The rate of recurrence of each word is a quantitative property, and we can look at the lexicon as a complete set of attributes.

Besides that, the text structure could be scarce in most attributes that assume 0 values. In addition, the rate of occurrence of the words may not be negative. As you can see, the structure of the text is unique and contains a relevant implication when dealing with computation similarity and mining algorithms.

Binary and set data

When we consider a multidimensional data that is binary, we represent it as a set-based data. This implies that a value of 1 means there is a component in the set. This type of data is popular in the market-basket domain where every transaction has information to determine if an object is present in the transaction. We can assume this as a special case of text data where the word frequency could be 0 or 1.

Temporal Similarity measures

This contains a single feature which will show time and other related behavioral characteristics. The temporal data may show a nonstop time series based on the present domain. The discrete sequence can be considered as a discrete version of the continuous time series. It is important for one to show that the discrete sequence data is not short-term since the contextual attribute represents placement. This is a situation common in the biological data sequence. The discrete sequence is also called a string. Additionally, a lot of the similarity measures applied in the time series as well as discrete sequence may be used again in other domains.

Chapter 5: Association Pattern Mining

A classic case of the association pattern mining is based on the case of supermarket data that consists of a set of items purchased by customers. This is called a transaction. The objective is to create an association among the items purchased by customers.

One of the most common models for association is the pattern mining which has a frequency of sets to quantify the type of association. The items discovered represent the frequent patterns or large itemsets. This field of data mining has different application areas as shown below:

1. The supermarket data

This was the initial inspiring point for the creation of association pattern mining. Moreover, it is the reason why we refer to the term itemset as the recurring pattern based on the context of items purchased by a supermarket customer. Determining items frequently bought creates an idea in the way in which items can be organized on the shelf.

2. Text mining

Text data appears as a bag of words. Therefore, the existence of a frequent mining pattern can help select keywords and terms that occur frequently. The repeated terms have a lot of application in the text-mining domain.

3. Dependency data type

The initial mining pattern concept has been interpreted into many dependency data types like sequential, spatial, and time-series data. These models are suitable for applications that use weblog analysis as well as event detection and software bug detection.

4. Other data mining challenges

Regular data mining can be applied in the subroutine to create efficient solutions to most of the data mining challenges.

Since frequent pattern mining challenges were suggested based on the market basket data, a considerable amount of the technology is applied in describing the data and the output borrowed from the supermarket idea. We can define a regular pattern as a frequency of a subset of all the possible sets.

Frequent itemsets can be applied in the generation of rules for association in this form X => Y where X and Y belong to a set of items. The most common example of an association rule that is common these days is the *{Beer}* ⇒ *{Diapers}*. In this particular rule, it is considered that if a customer purchases beer, there is a higher chance that diapers will also be purchased. In other words, we have a specific direction to the implication, which is created as a probability condition.

Association rules are common in different target markets. For instance, the supermarket owner might arrange yogurt on shelves that are close to milk and eggs. Similarly, the supermarket owner might decide to promote yogurt to customers who regularly purchase milk and eggs. The frequency model applied in association pattern mining is very common across many supermarkets.

However, the raw pattern frequency is not close to the statistical correlations. Thus, we have many models created for frequent pattern mining. We start first by looking at the frequent pattern-mining model.

Frequent mining pattern Model

The main weakness of the previous mining technique falls in the unordered data set. In this technique, we represent a set of transactions as T1....Tn. All the transactions happen in a database. Every single transaction is extracted from a universal list of items represented as U. We can express this universal set as a multi-dimensional record that contains a record of attributes.

Each of the binary records has properties to represent a particular item. The value of a specific record, in this case, is 1 if the item exists in the transaction and 0 if it does not.

Practically, U contains an extensive list of items compared to the normal items in the transaction T1. An example is the case of a supermarket database, which has more than a thousand products, in a single transaction; it will contain less than 50 products. This feature is associated with the frequent mining algorithm pattern.

An itemset represents a list of items. If we pick a k-itemset to represent k products, this will mean that a set of k items has a collection of items of cardinal k. Part of the transactions in T1...Tn represents a subset that creates a quantification of the frequency.

The association rule production framework

The frequent itemsets can further create association rules by application of confidence. Confidence refers to a measure in the association framework. For example, the confidence level of a given rule such as A=>B refers to the probability where a transaction can have a collection of B items.

Mining algorithms for a frequent itemset

In this part, we are going to look at several algorithms used in the frequent itemset generation. Since there are many different frequent itemset algorithms, this chapter will concentrate on a few popular algorithms.

The brute force algorithm

Consider a global collection of U items. This contains $2^{|U|} - 1$ unique subsets. Thus, one possibility is for one to create all members of the itemsets, and compare its support against a database of T. The brute force technique can be enhanced through an observation that the number of (k+1) patterns are popular with the number of k-patterns. Therefore, it is possible to count and enumerate support patterns that have one item, two items, and so forth.

In the case of a sparse transaction, the value of L is smaller than |U|. In this state, it is okay for one to end. If we want to boost the efficiency of the pattern-mining algorithm, we can use the following techniques:

1. Limit the size of the search space through pruning candidate in an itemset
2. Count each candidate support by pruning unnecessary transactions
3. Apply a compact data structure to represent the candidates

The Apriori Algorithm

This has a downward property which helps eliminate candidates found in a given search space. This property creates an open structure that depends on the collection of regular pattern items. In fact, data that is inconsistent to the itemset has to build a superset most effectively.

In other words, if we have an infrequent itemset, there is no need to measure the support of the superset candidates. This is useful if you want to reduce unnecessary counting. The Apriori algorithm creates candidates that have small length k and then count the support before it generates candidates of length k+1.

The final k-itemset frequency produces a list of k+1 candidates through the downward property closure. The production of candidates, as well as the support created in counting, exists in Apriori. Since counting a candidate is the major part that deals with the generation process, we advise reducing the number of candidates.

To describe the algorithm easily, we assume that items in the universal list contain a lexicographic sequence. This means that each itemset {a, b, c, d} may have a string of abcd items. You can apply this to create an ordering within the itemsets that have a similar order that corresponds to strings and may be present in the dictionary.

This algorithm will then start to count the support of individual elements to produce a frequency of 1-itemsets. This itemset is integrated to produce two itemsets whose support is already counted.

In general, the frequent itemsets of length K is used to create candidates of length(K+1) to increase the values of k. Overall, a frequent itemset that has a length of k is applied in building a candidate of k+1 length to increase the values stored in K.

We refer to algorithms that contain a number of support candidates as a level-wise type of algorithms. We can allow Fk to be a set containing k frequent itemsets, and Ck to represent a set of candidates that have k-itemsets. The basic concept basic idea is to generate candidates of k+1 repeatedly from a collection of k-itemsets.

The rate of occurrence of the k+1 candidates depends on the database transactions. If we generate k+1 candidates, we require the search space to reduce by determining if (k+1) candidates are present in Fk.

An effective support counting

To create the right support counting, Apriori has to analyze candidates in the itemset of the transaction exactly. This is realized when we use a hash tree in the data structure. The hash tree organizes candidate patterns carefully in a Ck+1 order to allow efficiency during the counting.

A hash tree is one that contains a specific number of internal nodes. The internal nodes have a random relation to the hash function, which will help in mapping the index of different children existing in the tree node. Every leaf node of the tree has a filtered itemset list. All the interior nodes have a hash table. For each itemset in the Ck + 1 has precisely a single leaf node of the hash tree. The hash function has to contain the interior nodes to help determine if a candidate itemset has a leaf node.

We can also assume that interior nodes have the same function, which results in

$[0 \ldots h-1]$. The h value is a branch of the hash tree. Each member in the Ck+1 itemset is translated into a tree leaf node.

Let us say that the initial point of the hash tree is at the level 1, and the subsequent levels rise by 1. Next, assume that the organization of items in the transactions is in the lexicographic order.

The tree has to be recursively designed from top to down, and the minimum count of the leaf node is kept by the number of candidates existing in the leaf node. Besides that, itemset contained in the leaf node are sorted in a specific manner.

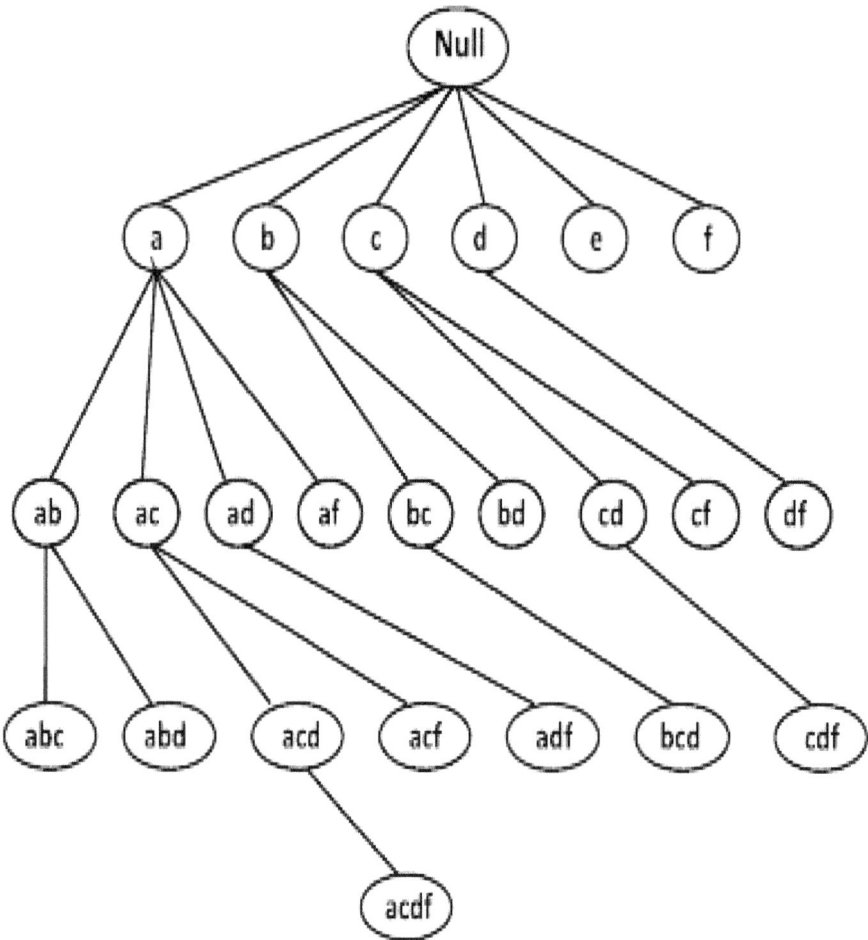

The Enumeration Tree algorithms

These types of algorithm depend on the enumeration concept. In this situation, several members of the itemsets are built like a tree. This structure with a shape of a tree is called a lexicographic tree. The candidate patterns are produced by extending the lexicographic tree. There are several ways in which you can expand the tree to realize different states between computational efficiency, disk access cost, and storage.

One of the main characteristics of the enumeration tree is to produce a theoretical representation of the itemsets. This kind of representation should depend on the constant pattern of the algorithms to ensure consistent mining of the member patterns. In addition, it ensures that the mining pattern does not occur in a repetitive manner. The result of these structures is the enumeration tree. We define the tree based on these itemsets:

> 1. A node existing in the tree similar to the constant itemset. The base of the tree resembles a null itemset.

2. You let I = {i1……ik} to represent a frequent itemset, in this case, i1, i2…ik are defined in lexicographic order. The itemset {i1…. ik-1} parent node is I. This means that only the child node can be extended with items that appear lexicographically. You can still view the enumeration tree as a prefix tree.

This ancestral kind of relationship creates a structure in the nodes found in the null node. Most of the enumeration tree algorithms operate through building an enumeration tree standard itemsets already defined in the strategy. In the first place, the root node has to be extended through searching for the 1-items. Then the same nodes are joined to form candidates. The candidates are then analyzed in the transaction database to find out the most frequent. The enumeration tree builds a framework that creates a structure and order in the frequent itemset discovery; this is created to enhance the pruning as well as the counting process.

Chapter 6: Cluster Analysis

In many applications, data has to be divided into smaller chunks. The division of massive data points into smaller chunks makes it simple if a person wants to summarize the data and derive meanings using data mining applications. An example of an informal but elaborate definition of clustering includes:

"Provided with a set of data points, partition it into groups that have similar data points."

This is an intuitive way to define clustering since it does not describe or go into detail about the many ways that we can create them. Some of these applications include:

1. Data summarization

In a wide domain, we can consider the problem of clustering as a way of summarizing data. However, data mining involves retrieving specific information from data. Usually, the first process applied in the data-mining algorithm is clustering. Therefore, many applications have the summarization property of cluster analysis.

2. Customer segmentation

It is important to find out common characteristics in a group of customers. This is done by differentiating customers. The most popular application of customer division is in the collaboration filtering. Here we find a common preference for a group of customers.

3. Social network analysis

Nodes bounded by a link have similar groups of communities and friends. For instance, clustering is used before the processing step in most of the classification and outlier detection scenarios. Models of different shapes may be used in different data types and situations.

The problem with a lot of clustering algorithms is that multiple properties are noisy. Therefore, these features have to be pruned so that they are not part of clustering. This problem is called feature selection.

Feature selection

The major concept involved in feature selection has to do with the removal of noise attributes. Feature selection is difficult to perform with unsupervised problems such as clustering. Another problem related to feature selection has to do with identifying an intrinsic behavior that exists in a set of properties. The feature selection method determines a subset of features by utilizing the pros of clustering. You will find two models that are used in selecting attributes.

1. Filter models

In this model, each score is bounded to a given feature that exists in the similarity factors. In this case, data points with a false score are excluded from the list. This model may show the state of a subset as a combination of a single property. These are important models because of the incremental effect of adding extra features to others.

2. Wrapper models

With the wrapper models, we have a clustering algorithm that determines the quality of features in a subset. After this, each subset is optimized in the clustering. It is a normal approach where many features rely on the clusters. At one point, the features selected will depend on a given methodology applied in the clustering. Even though this might look like a big problem, the thing is that different methods of clustering can work with a unique set of properties. Therefore, the methodology permits one to utilize highlighted properties in a given clustering approach.

In the filter models, there is a particular criterion applied when it comes to assessing the effect of specific features or a subset of features. Below is a brief introduction of the most common criteria.

1. Term Strength

This term is better applied in the sparse domains where there is text data. It is vital to identify both the presence and absence of zero and nonzero attribute values rather than distance. In addition, it is right to apply similarity functions rather than distance functions. This method allows one to sample document pairs and apply a random order between each pair.

2. Predictive attribute dependence

The inner motivation for this particular measure is the correlated feature, which will lead to amazing features. If an attribute is important, the remaining attributes can be applied in the prediction of the attribute value. We can use a classification algorithm to determine the property of prediction. In case we have a numeric attribute, we use a regression algorithm to model. Or else, we apply an algorithm to classify the attributes. The basic technique used to validate an attribute is illustrated below:

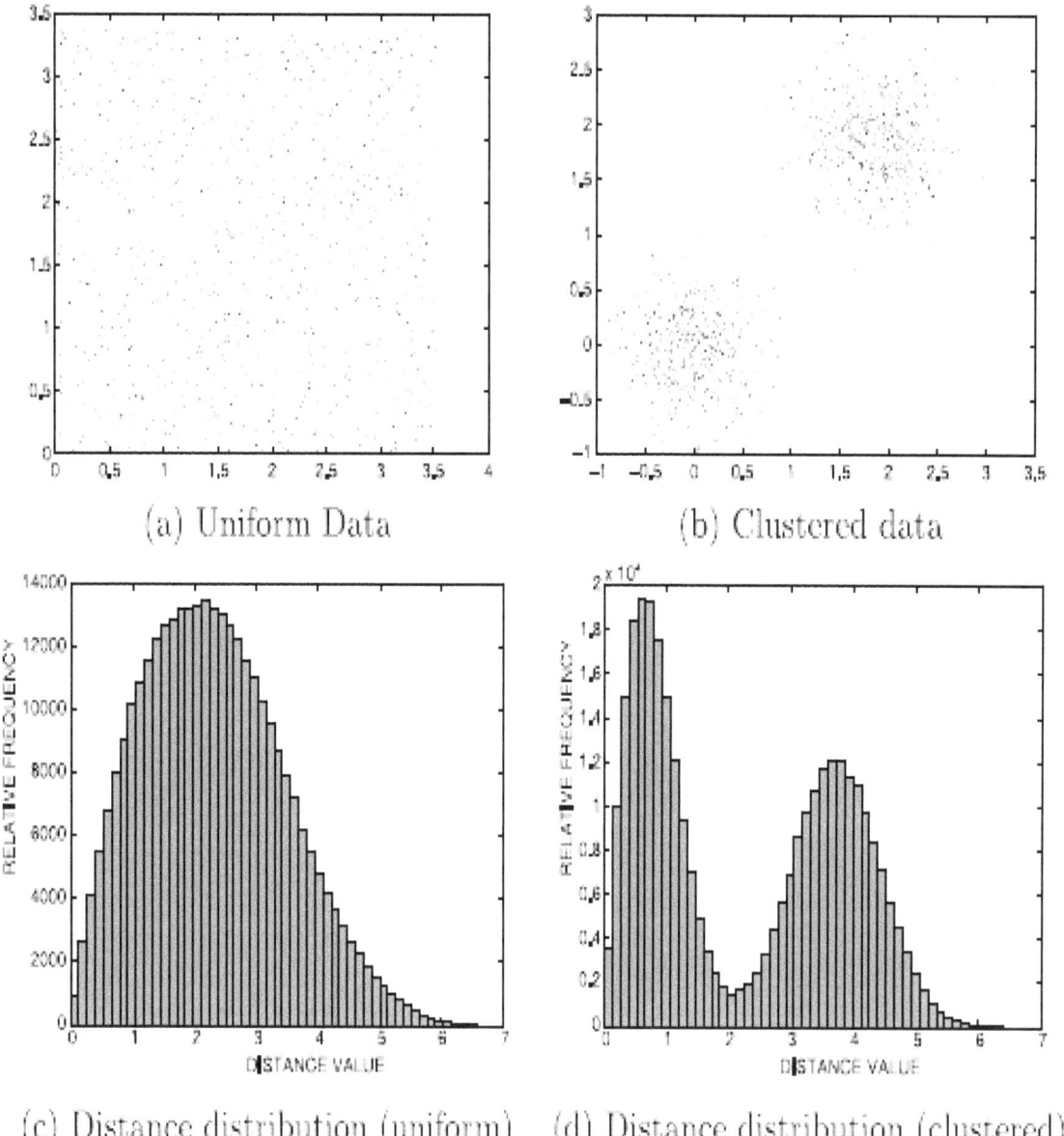

(a) Uniform Data (b) Clustered data

(c) Distance distribution (uniform) (d) Distance distribution (clustered)

    1. The use of an algorithm to classify all attributes except i is to forecast the attribute value.

    2. Report the accuracy of the classification in the form of a relevance attribute i

You can apply any valid classification algorithm even though a nearest-neighbor classifier is better because of the natural connections with similarity clustering and computation.

Entropy

The major point about this method concerns highly-clustered data that represents a few clustering features in the distance distributions. To illustrate this point, we can refer to the previous diagrams a and b. In the first diagram, we show a uniformly distributed data while in the second diagram we represent data that has two clusters.

The way a point-to-point distance is scattered has been shown in the previous two diagrams. How the distance is spread out in the uniform data is in a bell-like curve.

On the other hand, clustered data contains two unique points related to the intracluster distributions. These peaks will continue to rise when the number of clusters rises. The main point of measuring entropy is to validate the shape of the distribution distance in a given feature subgroup. Hence, these algorithms call for a transparent way of searching for a given combination. Besides validating the distance-dependent entropy, the natural style to quantify the entropy is through the application of the probability distribution on the points of data.

Presence of a uniform distribution with poor clustering behavior results in a higher entropy while clustered data has a lower entropy. In short, we use entropy to determine the feedback of the clustering quality of the subset.

Hopkins static

Hopkins statistic is applied in identifying the behavior of cluster in a data set although we can use it to determine a specific subset of attributes. We then use a search algorithm such as the greedy method to integrate the features.

Assume D is the data set with which the clustering tendency will be evaluated. We generate a model S or r synthetic data points in the data space randomly. Similarly, a model R that has data points denoted as r is defined from D. You can have a1....ar denote existing distance in the data regions to their closest members of the original database. Likewise, we let $\beta_1 \ldots s_r$ denote distances in various data points of a selected sample S to their closest neighbors in D. Therefore, we define the Hopkins statistic as follows:

$$H = \frac{\sum_{i=1}^{r} \beta_i}{\sum_{i=1}^{r}(\alpha_i + \beta_i)}.$$

The range for the Hopkins statistic is (0, 1). An evenly distributed data contains the Hopkins value of 0.5 since the values αi and βi are the same. Conversely, the value αi is going to be lower compared to the Bi for a clustered data. This brings us a value that is close to 1. In other words, a high value in the Hopkins statistic H represents a clustered data point.

Something to pay attention to is that the technique uses random sampling which means the measure can change as we move across different random samples.

If you want, you can let the random sampling be repeated several times. A statistical tail confidence test is applied in determining the confidence level when the Hopkins statistic value is higher than 0.5.

When we consider the feature selection, we can apply the average value of the statistic in many samples. This statistic is used to determine the quality of an attribute subset to help establish the clustering tendency of a given subset.

Wrapper models

In this model, there exists an inner cluster validation criterion integrated with the clustering algorithm to be used in the correct subset. The aspect of cluster validation is used to determine the efficiency of a cluster.

The basic idea is to select an algorithm in the clustering branch that has a subset of properties to explore and define the maximum combination of features. We can apply the greedy algorithm at the search space of subsets that have properties that could lead to optimization of the cluster quantification aspect.

Another technique to apply is by selecting individual features of a given selection criterion from a list of algorithms used to perform classification. In this instance, we have the set of properties examined individually instead of a collection of the subset. The technique in clustering sets up a collection of L labels having an equal number of data points identifiers.

Representative Algorithms

These are one of the easiest algorithms that depend on the distance to organize data points. This type of algorithms helps built clusters instantly, and the hierarchical relationships are not present in clusters of different size. Normally, this is attained through the creation of a collection of representatives to be used in the partitioning. The representatives of the partition may be applied as a function or selected from a set of data points in the cluster.

The central focus of the above methods is to help detect data representatives. When we create representatives, we use a distance function to create data points in their nearest representatives. In general, the number of clusters represented by k is defined by the user.

Let us take for instance a sample of data points represented by $X_1...X_n$ in the dimensional space. The purpose is to find representations of k $Y_1...Y_k$ that can reduce the objective function O:

$$O = \sum_{i=1}^{n} \left[\min_j Dist(\overline{X_i}, \overline{Y_j}) \right].$$

The total sum of unique distance points to their closest representatives has to be reduced. Do not forget that the allocation of the points of data relies on the chosen $Y_1 \ldots Y_k$.

There are different types of representative algorithms. An example of one is the k-medoid algorithms. This algorithm assumes that $Y_1 \ldots Y_k$ are extracted from the initial database D.

The k-means algorithm

When it comes to the K-means algorithm, the sum of the nearest representative is used to validate the objective function of the cluster. This gives us the following formulae:

$$Dist(\overline{X_i}, \overline{Y_j}) = \|\overline{X_i} - \overline{Y_j}\|_2^2.$$

In this case, the $\|\ this_p$ denote the Lp-norm. The Dist(Xi, Yj) expression is the estimation of a data point using its nearest representative. In other words, the general purpose is to reduce the total square errors in a given data point. This is also called SSE. In this case, it can be denoted as the maximum representative for every optimization steps existing in the cluster data points. Therefore, the variance between generic pseudocode and K-means pseudocode is the distance function.

A fascinating change of the k-means algorithm is the application of the local Mahalanobis distance. The application of Mahalanobis distance is important when we have the clusters expanded towards specific directions. The major factor builds Σ_{-1} creates a normalization point which essential to data collection of various density. This will create the Mahalanobis k-means algorithm.

The Kernel K-Means Algorithm

We can expand this algorithm to find clusters that have a random shape and use the kernel trick. The most important thing is to update the data that will generate shapes of random clusters to close the Euclidean clusters existing in the new space.

The disadvantage that comes with this algorithm is that it requires one to calculate the kernel matrix.

The K-medians Algorithm

This algorithm applies the Manhattan distance in the objective function. This means that the distance function *Dist(Xi, Yj)* is defined. In this case, it is possible to write it as an optimal representative of the Yj where the median of the data points in every dimension is the cluster Cj. One reason for this is that the least sum of the L1 distances is defined into points spread on a line of the median set. This shows that median optimizes the sum of L1 distances to the collection of the data set. When we have the median points selected independently along each dimension, all representation of the initial data is set to D. The k-medians technique sometimes is mixed up with the k-medoids that identify elements from the initial D database.

Hierarchical Clustering Algorithms

This algorithm clusters the data with the distances. However, the use of distance functions is optional. Many of these algorithms use clustering techniques like a graph-based method. You may ask yourself why these algorithms are that critical; the answer is that different clustering levels provide diverse application ideas.

This creates a cluster organization that can be identified through semantic insights. The best example to illustrate this is the organization of web pages.

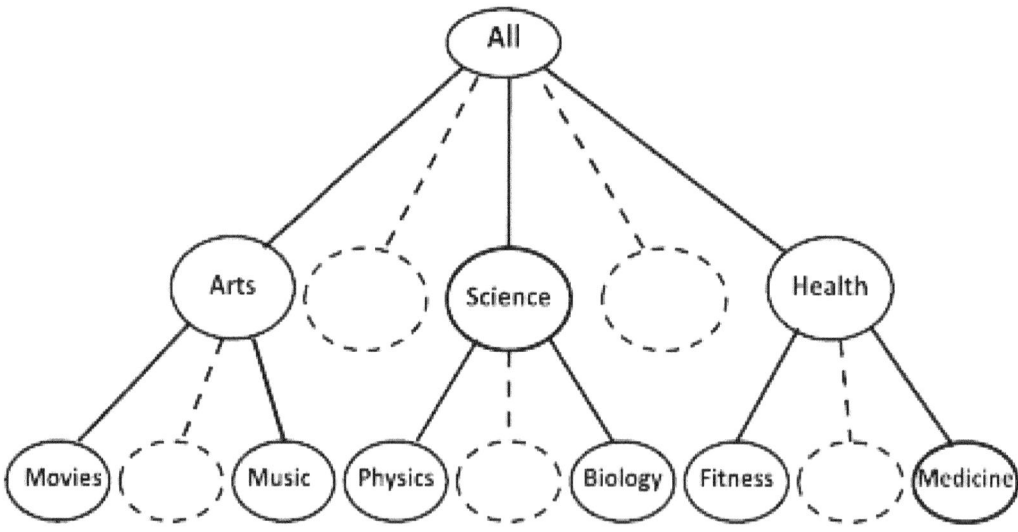

In the above example, clusters have been created manually. This diagram can help you understand the concept of multi granularity. Only a small size of the hierarchical organization is indicated in the diagram. You should see that at the top we have the web pages divided into multiple subject topics. The next level has the subtopics of the topics. Having this type of structure makes it easy for a user to browse. In other places, this type of organization occurs through indexing of algorithms. Besides that, these methods help create better clusters.

Hierarchical algorithms exist in two ways based on the structure of the tree.

1. Bottom-up methods

In this method, specific data points are subsequently combined to create higher-level clusters.

2. Top-down methods

This method partitions the data elements so that it appears like a tree structure. You can use a flat clustering algorithm to partition. This approach leads to massive flexibility concerning selecting the tradeoff between the point of stability in the number of data points and structure of the tree. For example, if we consider the growth strategy in a tree that creates a strong and stable tree structure same in all the nodes, it will produce leaf nodes that have different numbers at each data point.

Probabilistic model algorithms

Most of the algorithms we have discussed so far are hard clustering. A hard clustering algorithm is one where every data segment is assigned to a cluster. These algorithms are different from the hard algorithms; in this type of algorithms, it is possible for every data point to contain a nonzero assignment probability to all the clusters. A simple solution to deal with clustering can be turned into a complex solution when we assign a data point to a particular cluster.

The extensive idea of a generative model assumes that data has been created from point of k distribution using a probability distribution $G1…Gk$. Each of the distribution $G1$ represents a cluster of a variable component.

Association of EM to k-means

The EM algorithm has a different elastic framework to support the probabilistic type of clustering. If we can consider one instance of the Apriori probabilities p_i mapped into $1/k$ belonging to the model setting, and each element of the mixture has an equal radius in all the directions as well as the average of the jth cluster is taken to be Y_j. Therefore, the type of parameters for one to learn is the σ and $Y1 \ldots Yk$.

Practical Considerations

The major practical thing when it comes to modeling a mixture is the required flexibility of the integrated components. For example, once each component of the mixture is defined. It becomes simple to realize random shape clusters and orientation. On the other hand, this calls for an extensive number of parameters. If the data size is small, this technique will not work perfectly as a result of overfitting. Overfitting occurs when parameters on a small sample do not reflect on the correct pattern because of the instances of noise in the data.

On an extreme side, one can choose the Gaussian. In this case, each mixture component has an identical radius. The EM model works even if it is on a small data set. Moreover, the reason for this is that the algorithm learns only a single parameter. However, if the clusters contain a unique shape, this may create poor clustering regardless of whether the data set is large or small.

The common rule is to personalize the complexity of the model and correct the size of the data.

A large data set has a complex model. In some cases, the analyst may be aware of the domain knowledge related to the way the data points are spread out in the clusters. In this case, the right option is to find a component mixture depending on the respective knowledge.

Chapter 7: Outlier Analysis

In data mining, an outlier refers to a data point that is unique from the rest of the data. You can view an outlier as an additional aspect of the clustering idea. Even though when we deal with clustering we try to look for data groups that are the same, outliers refer to specific data points that are odd from the rest. We can consider them as abnormal, deviants or discordant in data mining. Outliers are used in many areas in data mining. In fact, the presence of outliers proves that a data set has noise. This noise might show up due to the errors committed in the process of collecting data. So having methods to detect outliers helps remove the noise.

When you are working on a particularly large set of data, you will surely find some outliers. This does not necessarily mean that there are data that you should be worried about. The larger the data set, the more likely it is that there will be outliers just because there is so much information. However, it is still important that you take a look at the outliers, no matter how large your data set is. Sometimes the outlier will mean nothing, but other times it could stand for some important information that you need to check out. In all cases, checking out the outlier can help you catch many different things, sometimes fraudulent transactions and more.

1. Credit card fraud

Presence of an odd pattern in a credit card may hint at fraud activity. This type of pattern is said to be outliers because it is not similar to other existing patterns. A credit card company would be able detect if there are any credit card fraud going on. They would look through the records to see whether a customer would make the purchase or not.

For example, if the customer lived in Kansas and made all their purchases in that state, then it might look weird if they all of a sudden made a purchase in Mexico. This would be even more suspicious if the customer made a purchase in Kansas at 9:00 in the morning and then by 9:30, there was a purchase in Mexico. The credit card companies have a variety of tools that they can use in order to determine if the customer have actually made a specific purchase or not based on their past purchasing history.

2. Detection of a network intrusion

Traffic in many networks is seen as a series of related records. In network traffic, outliers are said to be odd records in a sequence of changes that are unique.

Most of the outlier recognition techniques create a prototype of regular patterns. These models consist of distance-based clustering, validation, and reduction of dimensionality. Outliers are defined as data points that do not fit in the normal model. The measure of an outlier in a data point is defined through a numeric value score. In the same way, many outlier detection algorithms create an output of two types.

3. Valued outlier source

This type of score validates the behavior of data point considered as an outlier. Higher score values in the data point are likely to be an outlier. A few algorithms might display the probability value that validates the chances of a specific point of data in an outlier.

4. Binary label

This determines whether a specific region of data is foreign. The output has a few data compared to another as long as we can map a threshold on the outlier score to change it into a binary label. However, it is not possible for the reverse to occur. This means that unique scores are normal compared to the binary labels. Besides this, it is essential for a binary score to be present at the end of the result in many applications.

The creation of a foreign or outlier needs the development of a model of normal patterns. Most of the time, a model could be created to show a unique type of outliers depending on the restrictive model of patterns. These outliers have extreme values, which is important for a given type of application.

Below are the key models for outlier analysis.

1. Extreme values

We say a data value is extreme if it exists in both sides of the distribution in a probability. Extreme values can be said to be equivalent to multidimensional data using multivariate probability distribution. They are distinct forms of outliers essential in the basic analysis of an outlier.

2. Clustering models

This is yet another problem in outlier analysis. The previous methods search for data points that occur as a collection while this method looks for isolated data points. In fact, many of the clustering models identify outliers through an additional effect of the algorithm. It is still possible to maximize the clustering patterns.

3. Distance models

This model will search for the k-nearest neighbor in the data set to help identify an outlier. Generally, a data value is defined as an outlier if it happens that the k-nearest distance has a higher value compared to the remaining data values.

4. The density models

This model will first define the local density of each score. The density model is often connected to the distance model because the local density of a region is low when the nearest distance to the neighbor is large.

5. Probabilistic models

The probabilistic models have been looked at in the previous chapters. Since we can view outlier analysis as a complementary clustering problem, it makes it easy to apply a probabilistic model in the analysis of an outlier.

Information theoretic models

When we look at these models, we can identify an intriguing association with the rest of the models. The rest of the methods fix the technique of normal patterns and validate the outliers depending on the differences existing on the model. The information model will reduce the interval of the deviation in the basic model and select the differences in each space. If the difference is large, the point is then an outlier.

Pruning methods

We use the pruning methods when the r-ranked value is returned and the score from the outlier in the remaining data points is irrelevant. Therefore, we can apply pruning methods only for a specific binary-decision algorithm version. The typical idea when it comes to pruning is to eliminate the interval in the nearest k neighbor through the removal of data points considered outliers.

Sampling methods

We need to choose a sample of a given size from the data. Next, we determine the distance between two points of data in the selected sample as well as the one in the database. This procedure requires distance computations. Therefore, for every sampled point in S, we know the k-nearest neighbor distance. The first outlier in the sample is calculated, we can then estimate the other outliers using the first value.

The early termination Trick using Nested Loops

Most of the approaches that we have looked at in the previous section can further be enhanced through improving the next process, which involves finding the k-nearest neighbor in each distance of the data value. The most important thing to note is that to calculate the distance of the k-nearest neighbor of any data point X ∈ R it has to be followed by a termination once X cannot fall among the top-r outliers.

Density-Based methods

The density method applies the same principle as the density clustering method. The major thing is to create several regions in the underlying data to help create outlies.

Techniques of the histogram and grid

It is not hard to create a histogram to represent a given set of data. In fact, you will come across the use of histograms in many different applications. To represent data in the histogram bins have to be drawn, and then the rate of occurrence of each bin is determined. Data regions with a low frequency are said to be outliers. If we want a continuous outlier score, then we have to note down all the data points.

If we use an example of a multivariate data, we can generalize it using a grid. In the grid, each dimension is partitioned into equal width values. This is similar to the previous case where we assume the number of points in a given point as an outlier score. The data points contain a density less than T and can be defined using a univariate value analysis.

The biggest problem with this technique is that it is not easy to determine the correct width of the histogram. Wide or narrow histograms cannot represent the frequency distribution correctly. These problems are not different to the grid structures in clustering. Presence of narrow bins means normal data points fall into these bins in the stated outliers. Alternatively, wide bins will create irregular points of data and dense regions that can be combined into one bin.

The next challenge that comes with the histogram technique is that it is local in nature, and most of the time we do not consider the global nature of the data. One reason for this is that the grid density relies on existing points of data. Independent points may build an artificial grid of cell if the size of the representation rises. Besides that, the distribution of the density changes with the data locality, the grid-based methods might have some difficulties when it comes to normalization of the local variations in density.

Lastly, the histogram method fails to work correctly in the high dimensionality because of the sparse nature of the grid structure with the increase in dimensionality.

Kernel Density Estimation

This method is similar to the histogram techniques for creating density profiles. However, the difference comes in that instead of a rough model we get a smooth model. Using this method creates a continuous estimation of the density point. The density value of any particular region is found by adding the total of all the smooth values in a kernel function. Each kernel function has a width that defines smoothing levels.

The information theoretic models

Outliers are odd data not included in the data distribution. This means that if we compress a data set by applying "normal" patterns in the data distribution, outliers will change the length of the code required to describe it. You can look at the strings below:

ABABABABABABABABABABABABABABABABAB

ABABACABABABABABABABABABABABABAB

The second string has a length similar to the first string with one difference where it has the symbol C. The first string is also referred to as 'AB 17 times'. However, this cannot apply to the second string because it has symbol C. In other words, the existence of C in the string increases the length of the description. Again, you should see that the symbol above is an outlier. This principle is the basis on which we define information theoretic models.

Information theoretic models are similar to normal deviation models with only one distinction in the way the size of the model is determined. Typical models define outliers as a data point that is far from the estimations of a summary model.

We can look at the information-theoretic models as an additional model where several aspects of the space-deviation are reviewed.

Outlier validity

Just like in the models used to cluster data, it is essential that you find out the validness of an outlier that has been declared by a given algorithm. Even though clustering and analysis have a complementary type of relationship, it is hard to design the validness of an outlier.

Chapter 8: Data Classification

The classification challenge is similar to the clustering problem already discussed. However, in the classification problem, we learn the structure of a data set. Learning the different categories is achieved using a model. This model then helps one approximate the identifiers of a group. Some of the examples of input to a classification challenge include the data set divided into different classes. This data is called trained data, and the group identifiers are class labels. In many different ways, class labels contain a semantic analysis similar to the application.

The model learned is the training model; the previous data points that do not require one to classify are called a data set. The algorithm that is vested in the development of the training model to help in the prediction is called a learner.

In short, classification is also called supervised learning. One of the reasons for this is that a data set has to acquire the structure of the groups in the same way a teacher has to look over his or her students to achieve a detailed goal. Although groups acquired by a sorting model may have the same configuration of the variable features, it may not be available in each case.

When we look at classification, the trained data is critical to help map the defined groups. Most of the algorithms used in classification have two levels:

   1. The training phase

This phase looks for the training model from a list of a few training instances. This is illustrated using a summary of mathematical model drawn from the data group in the training set.

   2. The testing phase

In the following phase, we use the trained model to define the class label of the unseen instances.

The challenge in classification is much bigger than in clustering where we record only the user-defined grouping from a sample data. Classification is used to solve many problems. In each problem, there is a group defined based on the external application of a given criterion. Examples include:

1. Customer-focused marketing

With this one, the groups are the same as the interest of a user in a specific product. For example, a specific group may have a relation with the customers that are interested in a specific product.

In most situations, the training example of the previous buying experience is available. You can use this as an example of customers who might be interested or not interested in a specific product. The variable property could be similar to the demographic profile of customers. The training sample is important to help tell whether a customer has a clear demographic personality.

There are a lot of companies who would like to work with this customer focused marketing. Marketing in our modern world is complicated and expensive. Companies don't want to spend a lot of money making advertisements that won't go to the right people or ones that don't provide value to their target audience. Customer focused marketing would allow them to learn which products their customers are interested in so that the store is more likely to get the information that they need.

2. Medical disease control

Recently, the application of data mining in the medical research has rapidly risen. It is possible to extract the features from the medical records of a patient, and the class label may be associated with the treatment outcome. In this case, it is good to predict the results by using nodes.

3. Division and filtering of documents

Many applications that deal with news streaming need a real-time data classification of the documents. This is critical in organizing documents into specific topics in the web portals. Each sample document from a given theme may be present. The attributes are similar to words inside the document. A class label may include different themes.

4. Analysis of multimedia data

It is useful to classify large volumes of data such as photos, videos, and audio. Previous examples of user activities associated with a sample video may not be present. In this form of classification, it is essential that the trained data set be represented with n data points and dimensions. Besides that, every data point located in D is related to a given label. In some cases, the label is said to be binary.

In the remaining cases, the most popular convention is to assume that the label has been created from $\{-1, +1\}$. Then assume that the label is produced from $\{0, 1\}$.

A classification algorithm consists of two forms of outputs:

1. The label prediction

Here, the label is defined for each instance that is tested.

2. Numerical score

With the numerical score, we let the learner assign a total to each combined label that processes the intensity of the instance. One can change the score into a prediction label by either using a maximum or minimum value. The greatest benefit that comes with the use of a score is the unique test instances. This can be ranked and compared to a given class. These scores are important in situations where a single class is difficult, and the numerical score can organize the best candidates that belong to a given class.

One key difference lies in the way of designing two types of models when we use a numerical score to rank different instances. The first model has to account for the relative classification of diverse test instances. The second model requires the right normalization of the classification score of different tests. A few changes in the classification could be beneficial in dealing with ranking and case labeling.

Any time the trial data set is not sufficient, the efficiency of the classification model decreases. In this situation, a model could provide a detailed description of a random data set. In other words, these models may exactly predict the labels of cases used to create them. However, it does not operate well on hidden test samples. This is called overfitting.

A few models have been defined to help in data classification. The most prominent is the decision tree, rule-based classifiers, probabilistic models, and neural networks. The modeling process is the next phase after selection of features to help identify the most critical properties in classification.

Feature Selection

The first step in classification is the identification of features. Real data can contain features of different significance used to predict class labels. For instance, a person's gender is not important when you want to forecast a disease label like diabetes. Irrelevant features will possibly interfere with the classification accuracy model. In addition, it will also contribute to the inefficient computation. Therefore, the major focus when it comes to highlighting features is to detect and pick the most important attributes based on the class label. There are about three methods used in the feature selection:

1. Filter models

This method helps define the quality of a subset of features. Then we use it to remove foreign features.

2. Wrapper models

We assume that a classification algorithm helps define the way in which an algorithm may work in a given subset of features. An algorithm that searches for features is mapped to identify the right features.

3. Embedded models

The answer to a model in classification should contain hints associated with the properties. These properties are set aside, and the classifier maintains the features pruned.

Now, let us examine these models in detail:

Filter models

This model determines the features of a subset using a class of sensitive factors. The advantage of defining a group of features simultaneously is that it eliminates redundancies. Consider a situation where we have two variable features that are correlated with another where each can be defined using another one. In this situation, it is useful to use one of these features because the other one does not have any incremental knowledge.

These methods are much expensive because the second possible subset has features that require a search. Hence, a lot of feature selection method defines the traits independently from another one.

In fact, there are certain approaches to selecting features that build a linear pattern of the unique features by defining a set of new features. This method is similar to a stand-alone classifier.

The Gini Index

The Gini index is a statistical measure of distribution that was developed during 1912. It is used to help you gauge inequality in the economy and measuring income distribution. It can also be used in some cases to check the wealth distribution among a population. The coefficient is going to range between 0 (0%) or 1 (100%). Zero (0) is going to represent perfect equality and one (1) is going to represent perfect inequality. Values that are over 1 can theoretically happen because of a negative income or wealth.

A country that has residents with the same income would end up with a Gini coefficient of 0. A country that has one resident that earns all of the income, and everyone else earns nothing, would have a Gini coefficient of 1. Of course, most countries are going to fall somewhere in between the two.

This analysis can also be applied to wealth distribution, but wealth is sometimes more difficult to measure compared to income. This is why most Gini coefficients are going to refer to income. Wealth Gini coefficients are going to be much higher than the ones used just for income.

The Gini coefficient can help you analyze the wealth or income distribution in a country or in a region, but you should never use it as an absolute measurement of wealth or income. A high-income country and one that is considered low-income can end up having the same kind of Gini coefficient, as long as the incomes are distributed in a similar manner. For example, the United States and Turkey both have a Gini coefficient of 0.39, though the GDP per person in Turkey was less than half of the United States.

The Gini index is going to be represented through the Lorenz curve. This curve will show the income distribution by plotting out the population percentile by income on a horizontal axis. The cumulative income is going to show up on the vertical axis. The Gini coefficient is going to be equal to the area that is below the line of perfect equality, or 0.5 minute the area that is below your Lorenz curve, divided by the area that is below the line of perfect equality.

Though the Gini coefficient can be useful for helping you to analyze economic inequality, it does have a few shortcomings. The accuracy is going to be dependent on the type of data that you are using. Shadow economies and other informal economic activities can show up in every country and won't be used in these numbers. These transactions are going to show a large portion of the true economic production in many countries, but these show up even more in developing countries. Accurate wealth data can become hard to gather because of the popularity of tax havens.

Another flaw that you may see is that two countries could have very different income distributions, but then they still get the same Gini coefficient. While using the Lorenz curve as a supplement, your data can provide you some more information. It will not be able to show some of the demographic variations that occur among subgroups that are inside the distribution. This is why it is so important to understand demographics in order to better understand what the coefficient represents.

Use this technique to find the discriminative potential of a specific feature. This is used in the categorical variables, but one can divide it into a numeric attribute using the process of discretization.

Entropy

This is equivalent to the information gain. The measure of entropy achieves a similar target like the Gini index technique. However, it depends on the sound information. This entropy contains a value between [0, $\log_2(k)$]. A large entropy value leads to different classes.

Fisher Score

This score is developed to deal with numeric attributes and calculate the ratio of the average external distance to the average internal distance. A high fisher score results in a large discriminatory power. Fisher score is evaluated using the following formula:

$$F = \frac{\sum_{j=1}^{k} p_j (\mu_j - \mu)^2}{\sum_{j=1}^{k} p_j \sigma_j^2}.$$

The Fisher's Linear Discriminant

Fisher's linear discriminant can be observed as a summary of the Fisher score where freshly defined features relate to the linear arrangements of the initial properties instead of the subset of the original features. The path it takes is designed with a greater power of intolerant subject to the class labels. We can assume the Fisher's Discriminant as a supervised dimensionality reduction approach, which utilizes the stored variance in the feature space.

Wrapper models

You will realize that different classification models work better with various sets of features. The models of the features are biased to a specific algorithm of classification. Sometimes, it might be important to apply the features of a particular classification algorithm to help identify the features.

A wrapper model can maximize the feature selection process so that it can help the classification problem at hand. The standard technique used in wrapper models is to optimize a set of attributes frequently by adding more features to it. We can summarize that strategy into these:

1. Set up a collection of features either by adding one or more properties to it.
2. Apply an algorithm in evaluating the accuracy of the set features.

Embedded models

The major focus with these models is that the answer to many classification problems creates important signals concerning the correct features to use. In other words, the knowledge related to the features is inserted inside the solution to the classification issue.

Decision trees

Decision trees are a type of classification process that involves the use of a set of features in the trial data.

The function of the split criterion is to divide the trial data into more than two parts. In the decision tree, we build a partition using the training sample using the top-down approach. The only exception here is that during the partitioning, the criterion used in the partition has a class label. Examples of standard decision tree systems include the CART, C4.5, and ID3.

The following is a diagram that illustrates how a decision tree appears:

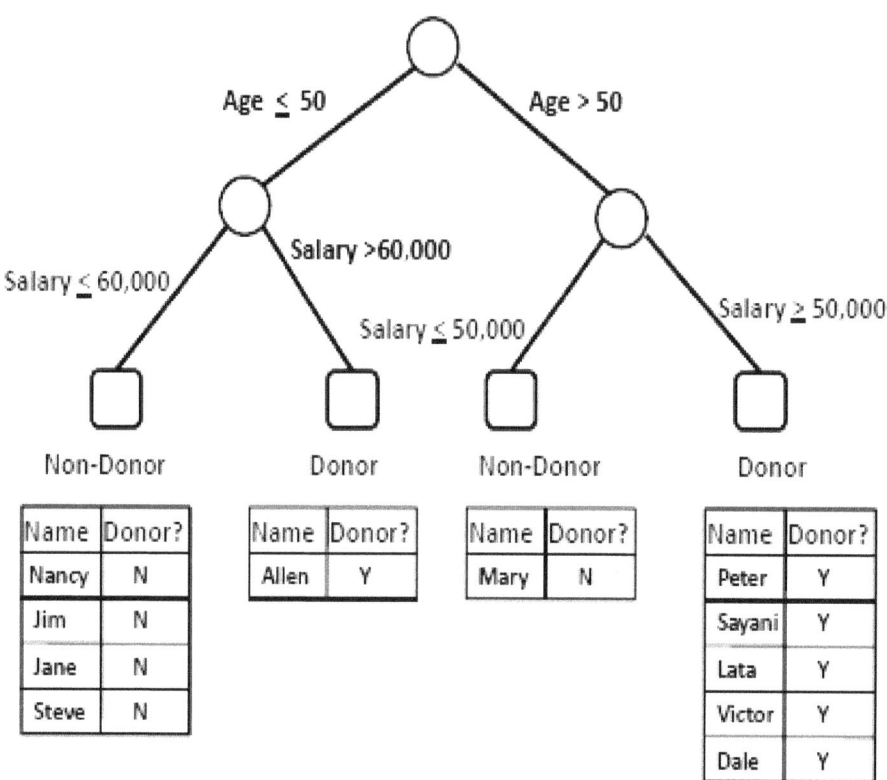

The plan of the split criterion relies on the characteristic of the attribute:

1. Binary attribute. This allows a single split and the tree will still be binary.
2. Categorical Attribute. In the categorical attribute, we have multiple ways in which we can split the tree.

Chapter 9: Applications of Data Mining in Business

We apply data mining in many ways in life. A lot of companies and organizations have impressed the role of data mining in enhancing their operations. Data mining provides a retailer with the chance to use the point of sale records to build a personalized feature for a given brand of customers.

Below are other areas that data mining is very important.

Healthcare

Data mining has the greatest potential to change the state of health systems. It uses analytics and data as a way to identify the correct practices that can be integrated into the health systems. This way, it reduces the costs and boosts the state of healthcare. By using the right data mining techniques, one can predict the number of patients in a given section. The processes are built to make sure that the right care is accorded. Data mining can further help in detection of underhand methods as well as abuse.

Market basket analysis

The market basket analysis is a modeling process based on the concept that if you buy certain items, the chances are that you may want to buy a related group of items. Therefore, this technique allows a retailer to know the best way to arrange their products in the store. In addition, it helps make the customer have an easy time while shopping.

Education

Another emerging field is education. Educational Data mining aims to predict the student's future learning behavior as well as study the effects of educational support. We can use data mining in a college to predict the outcome of students.

Manufacturing Engineering

Knowledge is what a manufacturing company requires. Data mining tools are critical when you want to discover patterns in a complex manufacturing procedure. We can use data mining a system design diagram to help create a relationship between the architecture of a product, product portfolio, and customer needs. Furthermore, you can use it to predict the time and cost of a product.

CRM

It involves searching for and retaining customers by enhancing the customer's loyalty and implementing customer-focused strategies. To accomplish the correct link with a customer, it is important for the business to gather and analyze the data. This is the point where data mining becomes important. With the use of data mining technologies, it is possible to use the data in analysis.

Identifying intrusion

Any move that can jeopardize the confidentiality and integrity of resource is said to be intrusion. The way to avoid intrusion involves fixing programming errors, information protection, and user authentication. With data mining, it can play a big role in improving intrusion detection by adding another layer of focus to the anomaly. It allows an expert to differentiate an activity from the frequent network action.

Fraud detection

A lot of money is lost through frauds every day. The traditional methods of fraud detection are complex and take a lot of time. Data mining can help create meaningful patterns that translate data into information. An efficient fraud detection system is one that can protect information about everyone. A supervised method consists of a set of sampled methods. These records are then categorized as non-fraudulent and fraudulent.

Customer segmentation

Although the traditional data may help one divide customers into different levels, data mining is far better in increasing the efficiency of the market.

Data mining places customers into specific division and provides the needs of the customers. The market focuses on retaining customers. Data mining will help create a brand of customers based on the weaknesses and what the business can offer.

The financial banking

With the emergence of computerized banking, a lot of data is created after every new transaction. Data mining can help one solve business challenges in the business sector as well as identifying correlations and patterns in the business information. The information can be of great benefit to administrators because the volume of data is huge.

Corporate Surveillance

The corporate surveillance involves tracking a person or behavior of a group by a corporation. The data that is collected is applied in the marketing purposes or even purchased by other corporations. This data can be important to a business that wants to customize the products to their customers. The data could be used in the direct marketing such as ads.

Research analysis

History tells us that revolutionary changes in research happen. Data mining is important when it comes to data cleaning, pre-processing and database integration. Researchers can look for and identify similar data from the database, which can create a change. The detection of similar orders and the association between any activities can be identified. With the application of data visualization, we can understand the correct view of the data.

Bioinformatics

Approaches in data mining appear perfect for Bioinformatics since it is rich in data. Extraction of biological data allows one to pick important knowledge from the huge data sets in biology. The application of data mining in bioinformatics involves protein function, disease diagnosis, disease treatment, gene interaction, and much more.

Lie Detection

Arresting a criminal is simple but getting the truth from a criminal is far much difficult. Law enforcement can apply mining techniques to carry out an investigation related to crime. The process aims to determine significant patterns in the data that is normally unstructured text.

Chapter 10: The Best Data Mining Techniques to Use

There are many different techniques that you can use if you want to work in data mining. Some of the major ones that you may want to consider for your next project include decision tree, sequential patterns, prediction, clustering, classification, and association. Let's take a look at each of these techniques so you can understand what they mean and when you can use them for your project.

Association

Association is the first data mining technique that you can work with. Association is used when you want to discover a pattern. This pattern is based on the relationship that occurs between any item that is in the same transaction as the other ones. Because of the relationship that is used with association, it is often called the relation technique.

You will find that association is going to be used each time there is a market basket analysis. Association is good at this type of analysis because it is able to identify the product sets that are commonly purchased together. They can then offer similar products to future customers in the hopes of getting a bigger sale. Retailers can also pull this information out to learn more about their customers to make targeted advertising campaigns.

For example, a retailer may find that many customers seem to purchase chips when they purchase beers, or cereal when they purchase milk. They would then consider putting the cereal closer to the milk, or the chips right next to the beers. This could save the customer time and will help the store see more sales.

Classification

Classification is a technique that you can use in data mining and it is based on the idea of machine learning. To keep it simple, classification is going to help you classify all the items that show up in your data set into one set of classes or groups. You get to decide what those groups are ahead of time.

When you work with the classification method, you will need to bring in a bunch of mathematical techniques to help you get it done. You may work with statistics, neural networks, linear programming, and decision trees. Also, with classification, you are going to develop a program that will help you automatically classify the data items into the right groups that you want.

Let's take a look at an example of how classification works. You can apply this technique to check out all the records of employees who have left the company and then use that information in order to predict who is most likely to leave the company within the next year (or another given time period). In this particular case, you would take the records that you get about the employees into two groups and you could label them as stay and leave. And then you can take the software that you are using for data mining to help you look at your employees and decide which of the two groups they belong to.

Clustering

Clustering is a great technique to use with data mining to make a useful cluster of objects. All the objects that are in the same cluster are going to have similar characteristics that allow them to be in that cluster. This technique will define the classes that you want to use and then will take all the objects from your set of data into each class. The difference between a cluster and the classification is that with clustering, the system will define the class and with classification, you get to define the classes.

To make this a little bit easier to understand, let's look at the example of how books are managed at a library. In this library, there are ton of books that come in about many different topics. The library has to figure out the best way to organize these books so that the readers will be able to find several books on different topics without a lot of hassle. Clustering will allow the library to keep similar books in one shelf together. The library can also add on some labels that tell the reader what that cluster is about. Then, if your reader wants to be able to grab a book in that topic, they simply need to head to that shelf and grab the book, rather than looking through the entire library in order to find what they need.

Prediction

The prediction method is a technique that will look for the relationship between the independent variables as well as the relationship between the independent and dependent variables. You may want to use the prediction technique when making predictions about future profits. The sales that you earn will be your independent variable and the profits would be the dependent variable since they rely on the sales. From here, you can make predictions based on the historical sale data of your company and come up with an idea of future profits.

Sequential patterns

Another option to work with is a sequential pattern analysis. This helps a company identify any patterns that are similar to each other in the data. It can also look for some regular trends that occur in time periods that you will specify. When we take a look at historical data and sales, it is easier to identify a set of items that your customers like to purchase together, especially during different times of the year. For example, during Christmas, your customers may purchase gifts and wrapping paper at the same time. This information is then used to help the company come up with deals for these products in order to encourage more sales.

Decision Trees

If you are working on a complex problem that has many potential solutions, then the decision tree is your best option. You will be able to write down all the possible solutions you want to work with, and then keep going down through the tree until you arrive at the best solution for your needs. Decision trees are easy to make, can work with as many solutions as you need, and provide you with a visual solution to any problem your company is facing.

Outlier or Anomaly Detection

Anomaly detection is going to search specific items inside a set of data that do not seem to match the predicted pattern or behavior that you are expecting. These anomalies are often called outliers, surprises, exceptions, and contaminants. There are many times that these anomalies are going to provide you with some actionable and critical information for your business.

An outlier is going to be an object that will significantly deviate from the general average that is inside your set of data or a combination of data. It is numerically distant from what you see with the rest of the data. This often means that the outlier indicates that something is different and that you should take some extra time to analyze it.

There are many times when you will use anomaly detection. Sometimes it is going to be used in order to detect any risks or fraud that occur in a critical system and these anomalies have all the characteristics to interest an analyst. When you find one of these anomalies, it is important to take the time to do further analysis to see if you can find out what is going on.

The anomaly can help you to find any occurrences that are out of the ordinary and could indicate that there are some actions that are fraudulent, that there are flawed procedures, or areas where a certain theory that is in use is invalid.

One thing to note is that if you are working with a very large set of data, it is common to find at least a few outliers because there is just so much information. While outliers sometimes indicate that there are some bad data, it could also be due to some random variations that could indicate that there is something important and interesting for you to look into. No matter what the case is, you should do some additional research and find out.

Regression Analysis

You can also work with a regression analysis. This type of analysis is going to try to define the dependency that comes up between variables. It is going to assume that there is a one-way causal effect that shows up from one variable to the response of an additional variable. Independent variables can sometimes affect each other, but it doesn't mean that there is a dependency that shows up in both ways, which is the case when you are looking at a correlation analysis. The regression analysis is able to show that one variable is completely dependent on a different variable, but it would not go backwards.

The regression analysis is going to be used in order to determine the different levels that may show up in customer satisfaction, how these levels can affect the loyalty of the customer, and how the levels of service can sometimes be affected by something as simple as the weather. The more concrete you are able to make the example, the better.

Often, you will choose to use two or more of these techniques for data mining in order to come up with the right process to meet your business needs. When you add these techniques together, you are able to get some great results that can really propel your business forward.

Conclusion

Data mining is the adoption of the automated database to store and analyze data that provides answers to business analysts. Traditionally, we used reports and query language to describe data as well as analyze the data. A user could develop several hypotheses related to a specific aspect and attempt to verify or discount it using a sequence of data queries, for instance, a business analyst who creates a hypothesis that people who earn a low salary and have a huge debt have a bad credit history. The analyst queries the database to prove or reject this assumption. Data mining can help one build a hypothesis.

As we have seen, the analytical methods applied in data mining are widely mathematical algorithms and techniques. The unique thing is the way the techniques are used. In short, data mining has many benefits in the present world. For instance, micromarketing campaigns strive to look for new niches, and the advertising industry has increasingly continued to look for prospective customers.

The long-term prospects of data mining are diverse. While this book has not looked at everything, it has covered some of the core areas in data mining. This serves as a solid ground to help you start your journey in data mining.

Next, you should look for advanced books in data mining and read more to help you master the concepts. Remember, you can only become an expert by reading and practicing.

If you found this book useful in any way, can you please leave a review for it?

Thanks for your support!

Here's another book by Herbert Jones that we think you'd be interested in

www.ingramcontent.com/pod-product-compliance
Lightning Source LLC
LaVergne TN
LVHW081518060526
838200LV00006B/212